"Lydia Jaeger's threefold competence could be forbidding: scientific (advanced studies in physics from Cologne University), philosophical, and theological. And yet, she manages to establish a warm contact with readers of many fields and locations in life—to feed their hunger for meaning without dodging difficulties. As I read this book, I marveled at the wisdom of the stance and the wording, even on rather sensitive issues."

—HENRI A. G. BLOCHER, Faculté Libre de
Théologie Evangélique

"This book, on how taking the biblical teaching on creation seriously will enrich our lives, is a delight to read. Behind the friendly and engaging style—full of good sense and clear Christian commitment—lies a great deal of deep and careful reflection. You will enjoy Professor Jaeger's company as she leads you to a fuller love for your Creator and for his creation."

—C. JOHN COLLINS, Covenant Theological Seminary

"Jaeger guides us beyond simply understanding the distinctions between world views that a biblical doctrine of creation marks out. With clarity and elegance, she moves the heart to appreciate the real-life implications that belief in a transcendent Creator-God entails. As much as I have studied and taught on this topic, every chapter contains some nuance I had never before considered."

—JOHN W. HILBER, McMaster Divinity College

"Here is a doctrine of creation that focuses—rightly in my opinion—less on origins than on ongoings, namely, the practical consequences of our createdness for everyday human existence. Jaeger argues convincingly that human flourishing, in every aspect of our lives, depends entirely on living in dependence on God, and along the grain of the created order. *Ordinary Splendor* confirms Calvin's belief that there is no knowledge of what it is to be human without knowledge of God the Creator."

—KEVIN J. VANHOOZER, Trinity Evangelical Divinity School

"Lydia Jaeger's *Ordinary Splendor* sets the tone on the first pages, when she opens the book with prayer. And her concern for 'living in God's creation' (and not merely thinking about it) remains throughout, as she engages topics like gratitude, procreation, and obedience, among others. Jaeger moves seamlessly between thought and practice, ancient and contemporary issues, biblical conviction and cultural engagement, in this timeless yet also quite timely work on the gracious gift that God has given to us and what kind of life that demands of us. I continue to learn from Professor Jaeger, and I'm always impressed with her balance of biblical certainty and grace. This book is no exception."

—GEOFFREY H. FULKERSON, Dordt University

ORDINARY SPLENDOR

Living in God's Creation

ORDINARY SPLENDOR

SPLENDOR

Living in God's Creation

Lydia Jaeger

Translated by Jonathan Vaughan

LEXHAM PRESS

Ordinary Splendor: Living in God's Creation

Copyright 2023 Lydia Jaeger

Lexham Press, 1313 Commercial St., Bellingham, WA 98225
LexhamPress.com

This publication was made possible through the support of a grant from Templeton Religion Trust. The opinions expressed in this publication are those of the author and do not necessarily reflect the views of Templeton Religion Trust.

Cover art is *Mountainscape* (1832) by Ernst Fries.

Print ISBN 9781683596998
Digital ISBN 9781683597001
Library of Congress Control Number 2022947473

Lexham Editorial: Todd Hains, Danielle Burlaga, Mandi Newell
Cover Design: Joshua Hunt, Tyssul Patel
Typesetting: Abigail Stocker

Dedicated to

Romainville Evangelical Protestant Church (France)

CONTENTS

Prayer to Our Creator   xi

Preface   xiii

I   *Recognizing God as the Absolute Origin*   1

II   *Accepting Existence as a Gift*   13

III   *Inhabiting an Existing Order*   25

IV   *Understanding Human Dignity*   43

V   *Entering into God's Blessing*   61

VI   *Obeying God's Commandment*   83

VII   *Accepting Your Limits*   97

VIII   *Distinguishing between Woman and Man*   111

IX   *Embracing a Fully Human Sexuality*   131

X   *Entering into God's Rest*   145

Epilogue   161

Study Questions   165

Bibliography   171

Notes   175

Subject & Author Index   181

Scripture Index   185

PRAYER TO OUR CREATOR

You are worthy, our Lord and God,
to receive glory and honor and power,
for you created all things,
and by your will they were created
and have their being.   *Revelation 4:11 NIV*

Almighty Father,
By your word you made the universe from nothing,
and its orderly structures display your matchless wisdom.
Grant that as we contemplate the work of your hands,
we may daily heed the teachings of your word,
rightly appreciate the privilege of being your image,
humbly accept the place you have assigned to us,
gratefully receive the good gifts of your creation,
and joyfully worship and serve you,
our transcendent Creator,
through Christ Jesus our Lord.

Amen.

PREFACE

A LARGE NUMBER OF CHRISTIAN CREEDS begin with the declaration that God is the Creator. To cite just one particularly well-known example, the Apostles' Creed opens with a declaration of faith in the Creator God—"I believe in God, the Father Almighty, Creator of heaven and earth"—and over the centuries, many other summaries of the Christian faith have followed its example. Acknowledging God as Creator implies, as the other side of the same truth, a second belief that is just as essential, although perhaps less often explicitly affirmed: all other beings are created by God; they are *creatures*. Thus, the Christian worldview is characterized by a fundamental asymmetry: creation, possessing its own solidity, exists face-to-face with its Creator, on whom all things depend, and who does not depend on anything. Just as the fact that God is Creator is decisive for the biblical understanding of God, so also the created nature of the world determines the way that we should look at the universe—and the way we should look at ourselves, since we are part of creation.

But what exactly are we saying when we declare that the world is created? For many, studying the doctrine of creation is limited to considering how it interacts with scientific theories about the origins of the universe and of life. We ask questions like: Does the Big Bang correspond to the first moment of creation? Do the biblical accounts contradict the theory of evolution? Can we accept that humanity, created in God's image according to Genesis, is the cousin of apes? Such questions are not unimportant; indeed, they need to be addressed by believers who are unwilling to separate their faith from reason, their Bible reading from rational thought. However, one would be wrong to limit the understanding of creation to these questions alone. These concerns admittedly constitute one stage in the interpretation of the Bible's origin stories, but they cannot be the end goal. Creation is an element that structures all that the Bible teaches us about God, about the world, and about humanity. A clear understanding of this key component of the biblical worldview is therefore essential for the Christian life: far from being of interest only to those involved in debates on science and faith, the doctrine of creation concerns all believers.

The following pages deliberately put aside, on the whole, the consideration of scientific theories about origins, since all too often this aspect tends to dominate, leaving little room to appreciate how much light the doctrine of creation sheds on reality. Instead, our aim is to take a closer look at the Bible's teaching on creation in order to explore its practical implications. Too rarely do we think about creation from the angle of everyday life. Yet we will only truly understand the declaration of God as Creator and the creation of the world if we perceive how it changes the way we live in the world, the way we relate to others, and the way we pray. The doctrine of creation is not a theoretical belief: those who genuinely appropriate it will find it has a profound influence on their spirituality and daily life.

This book is an attempt to draw out practical conclusions from my research on the doctrine of creation, undertaken as part of a PhD in philosophy at the Sorbonne. I am indebted to the many people who encouraged me to go beyond a purely academic treatment and consider the practical implications. In particular, I would like to thank the director of the *Institut Biblique de Nogent-sur-Marne*, Jacques Blocher, who challenged me to present some of the results of my PhD thesis at a spiritual retreat in September 2005[1]; Emile Nicole, dean of the *Faculté Libre de Théologie Evangélique* (Vaux-sur-Seine, France), who invited me to teach on the subject at the seminary's summer school in July 2006; and the general secretary of the *Groupes Bibliques Universitaires* (the French branch of IFES), David Brown, who encouraged me to publish my work in their *Question Suivante* collection. Henri Blocher, Jacques Blocher, David Brown, Nicole Deheuvels, Victoire Yau, and Sarah Zborowska read the manuscript in whole or in part, and their comments were invaluable in helping me refine the content and shape of this book. Lise-Laure Nobilet and Gert van Kleef prepared the indexes. The John Templeton Foundation, through its generous support, allowed me to take time away from my usual responsibilities in order to bring the project to completion.

The staff of Lexham Press, and Todd Hains, in particular, walked me through the process of preparing the book for an English-speaking audience, exhibiting patience and enthusiasm along the way. Jonathan Vaughan diligently and skillfully translated the French original into English. The opening prayer, which he wrote, sets the tone for the whole enterprise beautifully.

Over the course of 2004 and 2005, I preached a sermon series on the opening chapters of Genesis at Romainville Evangelical Protestant Church (near Paris). The preparation made me reread these Bible passages more carefully, considering their relevance to today's world. It is a privilege for me to dedicate this book to that community of faith as a sign of my gratitude, both for allowing me to serve them through the ministry of the word, and for the witness of its members who, through their faith-filled lives, encourage me to pursue my thinking and research in an attitude of liberating submission to our Creator God.

I

RECOGNIZING GOD AS THE ABSOLUTE ORIGIN

◆

I

"I N THE BEGINNING, GOD CREATED the heavens and the earth" (Genesis 1:1). The opening line of Genesis ranks among the most well-known words in Holy Scripture, and even of all human literature. From the very beginning, the Bible presents us with the sovereign Lord, who by his word creates all that exists. Scripture does not start with a rational proof of God's existence. Nor does it start with humans thinking about the divine, giving their imagination free rein to come up with different hypotheses about reality before finally arriving at the concept of the Creator God. No, right from the start, we are presented with God's power to create—the God who, without starting from any pre-existent thing, brings into being the entire cosmos in which we live.

The familiarity of the words can hinder us from realizing just how distinctive, indeed even strange, they are. In fact, this short sentence at the beginning of Genesis constitutes a remarkable summary of what distinguishes the biblical worldview from all other ideas that people have devised concerning reality. The philosopher Claude Tresmontant compares it to God's calling of Abraham, father of the people of Israel, to set out on the adventure of leaving his kinsfolk and going to live as a foreigner in the Holy Land (Genesis 12:1): "As Abraham left his family and the land of his ancestors, so from this first step, biblical metaphysics leaves the metaphysics of the nations."[2] Abraham had to make a clean break with the customs and traditions of his homeland; in the same way, Scripture reveals, right from its very first sentence, a worldview that is radically different from anything we might find elsewhere.

HUMANS HAVE ALWAYS PONDERED THE question of origins and have come up with widely differing explanations. At the time of Genesis's first readers, the most common answer was polytheism. This is why ancient cosmogonies not only recount the origin of the world, but also how the gods were born. The Babylonian creation story provides a striking example. Known as Enuma Elish, after its opening words, this impressive mythological text was probably written in the twelfth century BC; the whole work is in praise of Marduk, Babylon's principal deity. Here, water is presented as the origin of all that exists. Fresh water is the male primal being (called Apsû), salt water the female (called Tiāmat). The gods come into being in successive generations, from the mixing of these primeval waters. However, the parents are vexed by their turbulent offspring; first the Father, then the Mother, attempt to do away with them. But in the ensuing battles, it is Apsû who is first to be slain. Thereafter, Marduk, their great-great-grandson, comes to the help of the gods and kills Tiāmat. It is from the goddess's corpse that Marduk creates the visible universe.

Some elements of the Babylonian epic are also present in the biblical account: the essential role of water, and the placing of the heavenly expanse, for example. After all, both stories come from the ancient Near East and pertain to the formation of the world, of which sky, sea, and dry land are elements that no one can miss. But one does not need to be a specialist in ancient texts to recognize that the Babylonians' conceptual universe is so far removed from the atmosphere we detect in the biblical origin accounts. Rather than recounting the genesis of a multitude of gods, Scripture presents us with the eternal God who has no rivals. Instead of narrating a struggle between feuding deities, Genesis shows God establishing order in his creation; nothing and no one can stand in his way: "And God said, 'Let there be light,' and there was light"

(Genesis 1:3). Instead of forging the world out of a deity's remains, the Bible avoids any confusion between God and creation: the world, in its entirety, is brought forth by God's word, without incorporating any element of divine nature. Even when Genesis 2 speaks of God breathing into the man the breath of life, it carefully avoids the common term for "spirit" (*rûaḥ*), in order to rule out any confusion between God's Spirit and the human spirit (Genesis 2:7).

Admittedly, ancient creation myths no longer function as the framework for understanding the origin of our world. Science has, for many people, taken their place as an explanatory framework. It is therefore not uncommon to see scientific theories about the origin of life and the universe invested with a quasi-religious function: not only are they supposed to tell us how different forms of existence have evolved; they are expected to be able to disclose their absolute origin, reveal the meaning of life, and suggest norms for human behavior.

Using—or should we say abusing—science in this way is to forget, however, that the true aim of science is more modest. It seeks to study the workings of the natural order, precisely by assuming its existence and the laws it comprises. For this reason, science is unable to answer the time-worn metaphysical question, "Why is there something rather than nothing?" because science always studies that which exists, the latter having already been assumed as a premise of scientific inquiry.

◆ ◆ ◆

Marduk creates the heavens and the earth

When the heavens above did not exist,
And earth beneath had not come into being—
There was Apsû, the first in order, their begetter,
And demiurge Tiāmat, who gave birth to them all;
They had mingled their waters together ...
When not one of the gods had been formed
Or had come into being, when no destinies had been
    decreed,
The gods were created within them ...
Bēl rested, surveying the corpse,
In order to divide the lump by a clever scheme.
He split her into two like a dried fish:
One half of her he set up and stretched out as the
    heavens. ...
He put her head in position and poured out ...
He opened the abyss and it was sated with water.
From her two eyes he let the Euphrates and Tigris flow.

ENUMA ELISH[3]

◆ ◆ ◆

In the same way, we are going beyond the legitimate bounds of scientific research when we ponder the validity of the laws of nature themselves: one should not expect science to produce, as one of its results, an explanation of these laws, since any scientific practice is already founded on the postulate that nature is structured and unified by these laws.

Science is even less qualified to inform us about the meaning of life or morality: judging the aims or norms of human existence is not part of what science is equipped to do. Science seeks to describe what *is*; it is not competent to decide what *should* be. Thus, it can help us to discern if a given event did indeed take place and the precise way in which it occurred. But it is incapable of saying anything about the event's moral significance. The simple fact that an event occurred does not decide its value: in the court of science, crimes and virtuous acts are considered in exactly the same way, as simply *factual* events.

Too often the limits of the scientific method are forgotten, such that science is expected to provide an all-encompassing explanation of reality. This kind of inflated trust in science's power grants the universe an absolute autonomy: this world must provide its own explanation, by means of theories that never appeal to any reality that is beyond scientific description. This sort of dogmatic scientism rejects the very idea of imagining anything that falls outside the interpretative perspective imposed by science. As a result, the world takes on quasi-divine status: it has no transcendent foundation, but rather owes its existence to itself. This is perhaps not so far removed from the ancient myths in which the world emerged out of divine debris.

THE BIBLE'S FIRST SENTENCE CONSTITUTES A POWERFUL rebuttal of any conception, be it ancient or modern, that fails to make a clear distinction between God and the world. Of course, affirming that the world is created is in no way opposed to the scientific approach; in a certain sense, the latter finds its foundation in the concept of creation, since God creates an ordered world that is amenable to human exploration. In fact, the notion of creation demythologizes the world in a way that is conducive to doing science: a world that is infused with the divine encourages an attitude of passive contemplation and hinders the active approach that experiments require. So while science and creation are in no way opposed to each other, the Genesis account nevertheless rules out any quasi-religious use of science: the world does not explain itself, but has its origin and foundation in God. God alone is eternal and self-sufficient. Nothing and no one can ever rival him, since *everything* owes its existence to him.

The biblical prohibition of idolatry must be understood in this context, for this foolishness, according to the apostle Paul, is to worship and serve "the creature instead of the Creator" (Romans 1:22, 25). Revering something other than God himself, praying to someone other than God alone, would only serve to perpetuate the confusion between God and his creation. But let us remember that idolatrous worship can take many forms. It is not just metal idols we need to watch out for; mental ones are perhaps even more dangerous. For whatever is most important in our lives is, in reality, serving as a god. Not only can science take on a quasi-religious role, as we have seen, but any activity, or any person, who is the object of our deepest desire or our greatest fear, is shown by this very fact to be an idol. The majestic opening of the Bible reminds us that no created thing should usurp the glory that belongs rightfully to God; we are misguided if we hope to find anywhere else but in him the unifying foundation of existence.

The doctrine of creation not only prohibits us from directing our religious impulses toward the world; it also shows us how wrong it is to want to live without God. Even though many people live without God, claiming not to need him, the beginning of Genesis reminds us that this independence is an illusion. Even the most hardened atheists owe their life, and all that they are, to the Creator. Contrary to what anti-religious propaganda would have us believe, all people receive their existence from God. It follows that human life only acquires its true meaning when we are receptive to the existence of God. Only when we consciously accept our dependence on the Creator do we understand reality for what it is: created by God. In doing so, our life finds its center in prayer and worship, directed to the Creator, the origin of all that exists: "You shall worship the Lord your God, and him alone shall you serve" (Matthew 4:10).

II

ACCEPTING
EXISTENCE
AS A GIFT

◆

II

VERY FEW PEOPLE TODAY CONSIDER the world to be *necessary*; the instinctive feeling that the world might not have existed (or could have been different from what it is) is a powerful one. When one asks why the world exists, it therefore seems rather unsatisfactory to answer with its supposed necessity: certainly, the assertion that the world exists because it couldn't *not* exist does not ring true. One of the classic proofs of God's existence takes as its starting point the contingent (that is, non-necessary) character of the world, before tracing back to its necessary foundation: the third of Thomas Aquinas's famous "Five Ways" rightly affirms that contingent realities must depend on a necessary being.[4]

There does exist, however, an opposing strategy, which cuts short such an argument: one can refuse to wonder about the world's existence, if one considers that the world simply *is*, so that it is meaningless to ask why it exists. The 1948 BBC radio debate between the philosopher Bertrand Russell and the Jesuit priest Frederick Copleston is representative in this respect. The trajectory of the discussion shows clearly that the disagreement between the two men concerns not only the answers one might give, but just as much the questions that are pertinent to ask. Thus, when Copleston asks, "But are you going to say that we can't, or we shouldn't, even raise the question of the existence ... of the whole universe?" Russell replies, "Yes, I don't think there's any meaning in it at all."[5]

Russell's answer is in sharp contrast with the attitude that results when one believes in a created world: the fact of creation invites us to accept existence not just as a given, but as a *gift*. The reality that the world exists—or to put it more existentially, the fact that I exist—is not a meaningless fact, one which fails to stir any religious feelings. On the contrary, as the apostle Paul writes, God's "[invisible perfections], namely, his eternal power and his divinity, can be seen when one considers his works" (Romans 1:20). Creation bears witness to its

Creator; our contingent world does indeed point to its transcendent foundation.

Jean-Paul Sartre, in his novel *Nausea*, presents us with a particularly powerful literary expression of the opposite attitude. He fully acknowledges the non-necessary character of the world but refuses to infer from this the existence of God:

> The essential thing is contingency. I mean that, by definition, existence is not necessity. To exist is simply *to be there*; what exists appears, lets itself be *encountered*, but you can never *deduce* it. There are people, I believe, who have understood that. Only they have tried to overcome this contingency by inventing a necessary, causal being. But no necessary being can explain existence: contingency is not an illusion, an appearance which can be dissipated; it is absolute, and consequently perfect gratuitousness.[6]

This is the source of "the Nausea" that the diary's fictional author, Antoine Roquentin, feels:

> Everything is gratuitous, that park, this town, and myself. When you realize that, it turns your stomach over and everything starts floating about ... that is the Nausea.[7]

Sartre makes use of the traditional metaphysical categories of actuality and potentiality to express in precise terms his belief that everything is without origin. Medieval theology held that God alone is pure actuality. All other beings possess, in differing degrees, potentiality, to the extent that they could *not* be, or be something other than what they are: they are subject to generation, change, and disappearance. While not letting go of the idea of a contingent world, Sartre transfers the divine privilege of being pure actuality to the whole of reality: the changes that things undergo happen, it is true, without necessity, but they do not originate from a first cause that would itself be necessary. Thus, although the world is contingent, it does not depend on a transcendent foundation. In this scheme, beings can come into existence (and disappear) and nevertheless have no origin. One afternoon, Antoine Roquentin watches the wind blow through the branches of a chestnut tree:

> The existing wind came and settled on the tree like a big fly; and the tree shivered. But the shiver was not a nascent quality, a transition from the potential to the act; it was a thing; a thing-shiver flowed into the tree, took possession of it, shook it, and suddenly abandoned it, going further on to spin around by itself. Everything was full, everything was active, there was no unaccented beat, everything, even the most imperceptible movement, was made of existence. And all those existents which were bustling about the tree came from nowhere and were going nowhere. All of a sudden they existed and then, all of a sudden, they no longer existed.

... Existence everywhere, to infinity, superfluous, always
and everywhere; existence—which is never limited by
anything but existence. I slumped on the bench, dazed,
stunned by that profusion of beings without origin: ...
it was repulsive.[8]

Sartre's lucidity in his absolute refusal of God is terrifying: he
clearly perceives that deifying the world, as he has done, results
in the absurdity of existence. If we do not find our origin in the
Creator, we do not have "any right to exist"; our life is devoid
of meaning and direction, it grows "in a haphazard way and
in all directions."[9]

Nausea shows us that how we view the contingency of existence is not just a philosophical matter; it really does have
tangible repercussions on our attitude toward the world and
life itself. Does the world exist by itself or does it owe its existence to God? The answer we give to this question determines
the tenor of our lives: only if we accept existence as a gift
can we live gratefully. Those who acknowledge they are created grasp Paul's query, "What do you have that you did not
receive?" (1 Corinthians 4:7). They can therefore receive with
thanksgiving the good things in life, without a feeling of enti-
tlement or—perhaps even worse—that nothing has any value
or meaning. The contrast between the humble joy evident in
Martin Luther's explanation of the creed's first article, and the
indifference of Antoine Roquentin, for whom existence is a
loathsome burden, could not be more striking.

◆ ◆ ◆

"I believe in God, the Father Almighty, Maker of heaven and earth." What does this mean?

I believe that God has made me and all creatures; that He has given me my body and soul, eyes, ears, and all my members, my reason and all my senses, and still takes care of them.

He also gives me clothing and shoes, food and drink, house and home, wife and children, land, animals, and all I have. He richly and daily provides me with all that I need to support this body and life.

He defends me against all danger and guards and protects me from all evil.

All this He does only out of fatherly, divine goodness and mercy, without any merit or worthiness in me. For all this it is my duty to thank and praise, serve and obey Him.

This is most certainly true.

MARTIN LUTHER, SMALL CATECHISM, 1529[10]

◆ ◆ ◆

I am obliged to be

I exist by what I think ... and I can't prevent myself from thinking. ... It is I, *it is I* who pull myself from the nothingness to which I aspire: hatred and disgust for existence are just so many ways of *making me* exist, of thrusting me into existence. ...

My saliva is sugary, my body is warm; I feel insipid. My penknife is on the table. I open it. Why not? In any case it would be a change. I put my left hand on the pad and I jab the knife into the palm. The movement was too sudden; the blade slipped, the wound is superficial. It is bleeding. And what of it? What has changed? ...

That is half-past five striking. I get up, my cold shirt is sticking to my flesh. I go out. Why? Well, because I have no reason for not going out either. Even if I stay, even if I curl up quietly in a corner, I won't forget myself. I shall be there, I shall weigh on the floor. I am.

JEAN-PAUL SARTRE, *NAUSEA*, 1938[11]

◆ ◆ ◆

The reader of *Nausea* must, of course, remember that it is a fictional diary: it is uncommon in the real world to find individuals who follow through to such a radical extent on their belief in a meaningless world closed in on itself. But even if (thank heavens) the constraints of life often win out over complete consistency between philosophy and practice, *Nausea* sketches out for us, with a cruel but authentic directness, the absurdity at which one ultimately arrives when reference to the transcendent is done away with. Notice that it is precisely the (supposed) emancipation of the world from its Creator that makes everything veer into absurdity and turns the encounter with reality into "Nausea," since the world is experienced as subsisting by itself, as pure actuality. Thus, the "coup d'état freedom"[12] reveals its suicidal consequences: instead of conferring greater dignity on the world, the Promethean attempt to sever the world from its transcendent foundation ends up destroying its dignity. Creation has value only if it is acknowledged as being penultimate reality, as the work of the sovereign Lord. It has meaning only if one respects the relation that binds it to God, in its utter dependence. The world cannot bear the weight of the divine prerogatives: the idolater, who deifies a created thing, chases after nothingness. Indeed, he himself ends up resembling the nothingness to which he clings (Isaiah 44:9; Psalm 115:8).

III

INHABITING AN
EXISTING ORDER

◆

III

ONTRARY TO THE NIHILISM WE find in *Nausea*,
the doctrine of creation leads us to welcome
existence as a gift, with gratitude and joy. The
Bible's creation narrative allows us, at the same
time, to go further than the mere existence of the world. Not
only does the world exist because God created it, but more
importantly: it exists in a defined form, it is the *cosmos*, an
ordered world. Genesis 1 shows the creative act with a six-day
structure. This finely wrought account expresses the author's
conviction that he lives in a world with a well-defined structure.

The ordered cosmos of Genesis 1

In the first creation account (which concludes at Genesis 2:3), the refrain "and there was evening, and there was morning: the nth day" structures the work of creation into six days. Other expressions are repeated: "God said" appears ten times, as does "according to its/their kind(s)"; "and it was so" comes seven times. At three points in the narrative, the verb *bārā'* (to create) is used: at the beginning of creation, for the creation of the first animals, and for the creation of human beings. For the latter, the verb is even repeated three times, to bring out the special nature of humankind. This verb carries more weight than synonymous terms (such as "to make"), because in the Bible, God is the only one who creates (*bārā'*). Seven times in the story, God "saw that it was good." The whole creative act concludes with an intensified version of this divine seal of approval: "God saw all that he had made, and behold, it was very good" (Genesis 1:31). The story mentions three blessings: of the sea creatures and birds (the first animals created), of humans, and of the seventh day, the day of rest after the completion of creation. The great care the author takes in writing the story reflects his belief that creation gave rise to an ordered world: the finely crafted literary form expresses his awe and wonder at the beautiful and good order that the Creator has given to his world.

The six days of creation are presented in two groups of three days. On the first three days, God prepares the inhabitable spaces: on the first day, he makes light and separates the day from the night; on the second day, he separates the waters above from the waters below; on the third day, he separates the dry land from the sea. Then, over the remaining three days, he creates the inhabitants of these spaces: the heavenly lights on the fourth day, to guarantee the natural order of day and night; the sea creatures and birds on the fifth day, to inhabit the sea and the sky; and the land animals and humans on the sixth day, to inhabit the dry land. Each day in the first group thus has a corresponding day in the second. A small refinement of this two-part parallel structure underlines the strong link between the spaces and their inhabitants: some of the latter are already created on the third day, as vegetation sprouts on the same day that the dry land appears. We can therefore see that the first three days are not separate from those that follow; the work of creation forms a unity.

Not only is the notion of cosmos expressed in the six-day structure; it is also visible within the days of creation. Against all disorder, the narrative emphasizes the creative work that provides the basis for distinction: between day and night, between the heavens and the earth, between dry land and sea. This is the reason for the insistence that plants and animals are produced each "according to its kind." Likewise, the first chapter of Genesis does not describe the creation of humanity as asexual, leaving sexual differentiation to occur later, as some creation myths do. From the beginning, human beings exist with a distinction between man and woman.

◆ ◆ ◆

The conviction that we live in a structured world continues through the rest of the Bible. The Old Testament poetic books contain many passages on this theme. God's first speech to Job begins by comparing the act of creation with the construction of a building; it emphasizes the stability and precision of God's workmanship (Job 38:4–6). The Psalms exalt God's sovereign rule, which guarantees a stable order: "The LORD reigns; therefore the world is established; it shall never be moved" (Psalms 93:1; 96:10). In the face of his persecutors' hostility, the believer is comforted by the immutability of the natural order: "Your faithfulness endures from generation to generation; you have established the earth, and it stands fast. Because of your judgments, the whole universe stands firm to this day; for it is your servant" (Psalm 119:89–91). The hymn in praise of wisdom, in the book of Job, describes the laws that the Creator has given to natural phenomena in quantitative terms (Job 28:25–27; compare 38:25):

> He determined the weight of the wind,
>> And appointed the measure of the waters.
> When he determined a law for the rain
>> And a course for lightning and thunder,
> He saw wisdom and declared it,
>> He established it and searched it out.

Of particular significance is the Bible's use of the metaphor of speech in relation to the structure of the world. In the very first chapter we see the word giving rise to an ordered creation: "And God said, 'Let there be light,' and there was light." Ten times in this account, the author shows God creating through his word. Other biblical texts contain the same idea. For example, the psalmist celebrates the divine word in creation: "By the word of the LORD the heavens were made, and by the breath of his mouth all their host [i.e., the stars]" (Psalm 33:6). The prologue of John's Gospel alludes to the first creation account in Genesis when it attributes creation to the second person of the Trinity, referred to as the *Logos*: "In the beginning was the Word, and the Word was with God, and the Word was God. ... All things came into being through him, and nothing that has come into being came into being without him" (John 1:3). The anonymous author of the letter to the Hebrews states that the Son, the Father's ultimate revelation, sustains "all things by his powerful word" (Hebrews 1:3). Thus, the divine *Logos* forms the world and guarantees its rational structure.

The fact that the Bible sees the world as endowed with order is linked to its very conception of God. Creation bears witness that the Lord "is not a God of disorder, but of peace" (1 Corinthians 14:33). It is monotheism that enables us to conceive of this order as harmonious and universal. The Lord alone is God; nothing and no one is outside his rule. Contrary to polytheism, where no deity is almighty and thus able to command absolute obedience to their will, the biblical God is

◆ ◆ ◆

Nausea's world without origin or structure

Usually, strong and stocky, together with the stove, the green lamps, the big windows, the ladders, [the books] dam up the future. As long as you stay between these walls, whatever comes along must come along to the right or the left of the stove. If St. Denis himself were to come in carrying his head in his hands, he would have to enter on the right, and walk between the shelves devoted to French Literature and the table reserved for women readers. And if he doesn't touch the ground, if he floats a foot above the floor, his bleeding neck will be exactly at the level of the third shelf of books. Thus these objects serve at least to fix the limits of probability.

Well, today they no longer fixed anything at all: it seemed that their very existence was being called in question, that they were having the greatest difficulty in passing from one moment to the next. ... The world was waiting ... it was waiting for its attack, its Nausea. ...

I got up. I could no longer stay where I was in the midst of these enfeebled objects. I went to the window and glanced out. ... I murmured: "*Anything* can occur, *anything* can happen." ...

I looked in alarm at these unstable creatures which, in another hour, in another minute, were perhaps going to collapse: yes, I was there, I was living in the midst of these books crammed full of knowledge, some of them describing the immutable forms of animal species, and others explaining that the quantity of energy in the world remained unchanged; I was there, standing in front of a window whose panes had an established index of refraction. But what weak barriers! It is out of laziness, I suppose, that the world looks the same day after day. Today it seemed to want to change. And in that case *anything*, *anything* could happen.

JEAN-PAUL SARTRE, *NAUSEA*, 1938[14]

◆ ◆ ◆

sovereign over all that exists. In this way, he combines in himself attributes that are often dissociated: he is both wise *and* powerful. As such, no obstacle can prevent him from establishing the order that he, in his wisdom, has decided. By virtue of this, the acknowledgment of the transcendent God led the biblical writers to "see the universe as a unity, organized and internally related in all its parts, and permeated as well by a single will."[13]

Once again, Sartre's *Nausea* can help us to appreciate the gulf between the biblical worldview and the idea of an autonomous world, "without origin," which has no obligations to anyone or anything. One page from Roquentin's diary expresses, in a particularly striking fashion, what it means to live in an orderless world. That day, *Nausea*'s protagonist is in a library, where he experiences the head-spinning feeling of the state of existence cut free from any given structure. Once again, Sartre's description is notably radical: it is not unusual to question the existence of objective standards in ethics, but the author goes further and discerns that a world "without origin" cannot possess any veritable structure, not even one imposed by the laws of nature. For how can one conceive of a moral or natural order, without One to establish and guarantee it? Indeed, in his absence, "*anything* can occur, *anything* can happen."

Contrary to Sartre's perspective, the Scriptures stress that human beings do not live in a world that is devoid of form and can therefore be shaped to their liking. The structures established at creation determine the whole of reality in which human existence has its place. Thinking about the created order thus leads to many diverse applications. It should be noted, for example, that technical progress has enabled us to become much more independent of natural cycles than at any other period in history: daily, monthly, and annual rhythms have lost their predominance in industrialized societies. Of course, it would be a mistake to simply decry this distancing from nature; it has given us greater control over our environment and made us less dependent on fluctuating circumstances. The fact that Western Europe has not experienced any devastating famines since the middle of the nineteenth century is largely due to such technological advances, which allow higher agricultural yields, better storage, and more efficient distribution of food. Yet the ecological problems which pose an increasing risk to humanity's survival show that independence from natural rhythms comes at a price. The ecological threat thus forces us to consider the *moral* meaning of the created world's finely balanced state: the world is not simply as it is, its structures being of no value. The world's order is *created*; it is the outworking of a divine plan. Neglecting it, or even rejecting it, is therefore not morally neutral.

Of course, we should not be too hasty in drawing out the implications. But if we acknowledge the world as being created, we are obliged to consider the relevance of its structures.

Evaluating the morality of deviations from the created order is complicated by humanity's vocation to have dominion over the earth and cultivate the garden (Genesis 1:28; 2:15). It follows that humans are not simply subject to created structures, unlike the inanimate natural world, or even animals governed by their instincts. Rather, human beings are called to depend on the natural order, in order to shape our environment and flourish in it. Some kind of independence from creation's laws therefore seems inevitable in the exercise of our freedom; this is an indicator of human dignity.

Nevertheless, humans must not cross over into revolt against the order established at creation, on the pretext that God has given us dominion over the earth. Knowing when that threshold has been crossed, in each particular case, is no easy task. The following distinction can serve as a guide: we may accept actions that bring out some aspect of creation's potential, that extend and develop what was begun by the initial creative act. Moreover, mastery of the natural order, though always limited, can provide us with means to combat some of the harmful consequences that sin has in human lives ever since evil came and disrupted creation's initial harmony. On the other hand, we must reject any enterprise whose ultimate aim is to liberate us from the structures that God created.

It is often difficult to judge what constitutes a legitimate shaping of natural structures versus outright rebellion against creation's order. At what point does an acceptable use of medical treatment to augment the body's natural capacities, or cure a disease, become an encouragement for patients to seek eternal youth, or feed the doctor's desire for unlimited power? When is art in the business of refining nature, and when is it the expression of a desire to repudiate nature altogether? Although it is often easier to ask such questions than to provide answers in specific situations, we should nonetheless try to use our discernment. Neglecting to do so would open the way for various misuses of our powers, some with serious consequences. Some academics even believe that totalitarianism, with its goal of complete control of society and of individuals, comes from the "resentment of the fact that one is not the creator of the universe and oneself."[15] The dream of forging a new humanity, in the image of the *Führer* or the party, would thus be a particularly perverted expression of rebellion against our world's dependence on God. The atrocities that this dream has given rise to show with great clarity that human beings cannot possibly find happiness until they accept the natural order established by the Creator.

While totalitarianism can be considered an extreme form of rebellion against the created order, we must also be aware of the more subtle forms and various ramifications that this kind of revolt may take. The structures that creation puts in place are so fundamental that our attitude toward them has an influence on all aspects of human existence. Let us take an example from a completely different field from those mentioned so far:

our conception of human knowledge. It is quite commonly affirmed that knowledge consists of our (admittedly partial) grasp of the world and its structures. We are convinced, in the sciences in particular, that our investigations enable us to understand reality for what it is in itself, provided that we implement, with sufficient rigor and perseverance, the tried-and-tested methods of controlled experiment and the construction of constantly revisable theories. Thus, most scientists consider that they are discovering (rather than inventing) the laws of nature that they study.

What might seem obvious at first glance actually proves to be deeply mysterious when we think about it: What guarantee do we have that human intelligence is suited to understanding reality? On what basis do we believe that our thinking is a reliable instrument for grasping this world's order? Einstein expressed these questions in his famous aphorism: "What will always be incomprehensible about the world is its comprehensibility."[16] Some philosophies have therefore developed a theory of knowledge that does away with any structure of reality: the world presents itself to our experience without any inherent form. Those who adopt this view of knowledge often cite the Scottish philosopher David Hume (1711–1776) whose work included a skeptical interpretation of the principle of causality: we consider that an event produces an effect simply because we regularly see the two events together, but the causal relationship does not exist as such. Roquentin's day at the library wonderfully illustrates a world where there are no laws objectively governing nature. One contemporary proponent of such an approach, the philosopher Bas van Fraassen, thus expresses the belief that we live "in a world governed by no laws except those we create ourselves."[17] In such a world, the mystery of human intelligence's adequacy for understanding reality disappears, since there are no structures to discover, in the literal sense. But along with the mystery we also lose that which, for many, underlies the whole point of knowledge: the desire to discover the world and its laws.

The doctrine of creation denounces as illusory the solution (or, should we say, dissolution) of the mystery of knowledge proposed by the Humean philosophers: if our world is endowed with an objective order, humans must calibrate their intelligence to this order that they have first received as something given. Our ability to do this is guaranteed by the common origin of the human mind and the world to be explored: the two correspond to each other, since they were created by the same God. It is therefore legitimate to hope that human reason is capable of grasping the structures of reality, albeit in a limited, fragmentary fashion. Of course, the human knowledge act is always secondary to the creative act that has shaped the environment which we inhabit. But we humans should not feel humiliated by the fact that our knowledge is derivative in its nature. For it is this quality which gives us the possibility of knowing the world: since human intelligence and nature are both created by God, there is a complicity between them which guarantees the adequacy of the human mind to understand the world we set out to explore.

The doctrine of creation leads not only to the rejection of the Humean theory of knowledge, it also stands against the revision proposed by Immanuel Kant. Realizing the difficulty of understanding the knowledge act without admitting the existence of some form of order, Kant suggested that the structuring instance was located in the human mind. He kept Hume's idea that the raw material of our experience is formless. But for Kant, human understanding structures this material by applying its own categories to it and thereby provides order: "It is we therefore who carry into the phenomena which we call nature, order and regularity, nay, we should never find them in nature, if we ourselves, or the nature of our mind, had not originally placed them there."[18] Admittedly, Kantianism in its original version now seems outdated, with its notion of human understanding having fixed and universal categories. But the fundamental idea continues to inspire several emergentist philosophies of science, in which the natural order is not so much discovered, but constructed: through experiment and the development of theories, we participate in the emergence of scientific laws, in a kind of partnership with nature.

Comparing Kant's philosophy with the worldview consistent with creation shows that ultimately, Kant grants the role of creator to the human mind. Indeed, instead of starting from the objective structures of the world, established at creation, he considers that our understanding imposes its categories on reality. Admittedly, he has, along with Humean skepticism, dissolved the mystery of knowledge: it is hardly surprising that the human mind understands the laws which it has itself added to the formless raw material of experience, since it is the mind which put them there. But again, the comprehension hereby acquired can hardly be called knowledge of the external world; it cannot grasp any natural order that exists prior to the knowledge act. On the other hand, if the creation is structured by God's word, then human beings are not creators, but only "finite reinterpreter[s]"[19] of the natural order. Humans are faced with "the gift [of being] that marks the *exteriority* of the provenance. ... The theologian must remain a 'realist' insofar as what is created can only truly appear via a *mediation of being*, a mediation that indicates both that creation has its own solidity *and* that it exists to point to a free self-positing that alone gives it this solidity, and its thickness, its reality."[20] Understanding the world as created by God's will means acknowledging its objective order. Humans therefore have the vocation of discovering it, even if our grasp of reality is always partial. The fact that we ourselves have not created this order to be explored necessarily limits our pretensions. But at the same time, our status as created beings underlies the very possibility of the cognitive process: human intelligence is at home in this world, since both were created by God, the source of all rationality.

IV

UNDERSTANDING
HUMAN DIGNITY

◆

IV

*I*N THE MESOPOTAMIAN EPIC *Atrahasis*, the lesser gods resent the heavy workload imposed on them by the higher gods. To avoid conflict and ensure the work still gets done, human beings are created, so that they can labor instead of the gods. When we compare this myth with the biblical narrative, the contrast could not be more striking: "The God who created the world and all that is in it, who is Lord over heaven and earth ... is not served by human hands, as though he lacked anything, he who gives to all people life and breath and all things" (Acts 17:24–25). There

◆ ◆ ◆

The gods create humans to do their work for them

When the gods instead of man
Did the work, bore the loads,
The gods' load was too great,
The work too hard, the trouble too much,
The great *Anunnaki* [the chief gods] made the *Igigi*
    [the worker gods]
Carry the workload sevenfold. ...
They[21] were counting the years of loads.
For 3,600 years they bore the excess,
Hard work, night and day.
They groaned and blamed each other,
Grumbled over the masses of excavated soil ...
The gods ...
Set fire to their tools,
Put aside their spades for fire,
Their loads for the fire-god,
They flared up. When they reached
The gate of warrior Ellil's dwelling,
It was night, the middle watch,
The house was surrounded, the god had not realized.

The oldest and best-conserved manuscript of Atrahasis, *written in the 17th century BC by a certain Ipiq-Aya, contains a lacuna which prevents us from understanding the exact circumstances by which the gods dream up a solution to their plight. The text continues:*

Belet-ili the womb goddess is present—
Let her create primeval man
So that he may bear the yoke ...
Let man bear the load of the gods! ...
Enki made his voice heard
And spoke to the great gods,
'On the first, seventh, and fifteenth of the month
... one god should be slaughtered ...
Nintu shall mix clay
With his flesh and his blood.
Then a god and a man
Will be mixed together in clay.

ATRAHASIS[22]

◆ ◆ ◆

is no trace in Scripture of any need that God might have experienced and sought to fulfill by creating the universe; the sovereign Lord is fully independent of the world. While human self-sufficiency (or more accurately, the illusion of it) leads all too often to withdrawal, the freely given nature of the creative act vividly highlights the generosity with which God calls his created beings into existence.

The two creation accounts in the book of Genesis express, each in its own way, the care that God demonstrates when humans are created. The first (Genesis 1:1–2:3) places the creation of human beings right at the end of the creation week. The biblical author in no way suggests that God might depend on human work; quite the opposite: not only does God provide food for humans and for the animals (Genesis 1:29–30), but the creation of humans is closely followed by the Sabbath rest that marks the completion of the creative endeavor (Genesis 2:1–3). In the second account (Genesis 2), God prepares a place for humankind, "a garden in Eden" (Genesis 2:8). The Hebrew word ʿēden means "delight" and suggests a pleasant existence, a luxurious life. The way the place is described matches its name perfectly: the garden contains "every tree that is pleasant to the eye and good for food" (Genesis 2:9); it is both a park and an orchard. It fully satisfies not only humanity's material needs, but also the longing for beauty. The abundant irrigation guarantees fertile soil: an immense river with four great branches waters Eden. One can imagine the flow of a river two of whose branches are among the most important rivers in the world: the Euphrates and the Tigris.[23] It is true that the power of water can be devastating, as the account of the flood will show. Up to the present day, humans have been unable to tame the fury of floods and tsunamis. But in Eden, water's power is a force for good: it irrigates and gives life; it means humans can fulfill their task of cultivating the garden.

Since God does so much to prepare an environment fit for humans, we can conclude that they have a privileged status. Both creation accounts pay special attention to human beings, but the second one especially focuses on the human condition. Right from its opening verse, we see a reversal of the order of the heavens and the earth, which doubtlessly indicates a special focus on the earthly sphere (Genesis 2:4):

> This is the "offspring" of the heavens and earth when they were created,
> In the day that the LORD God made the earth and the heavens.

As a result, the man—the "earthling," as the name "Adam," which comes from the Hebrew word for "ground, earth," indicates—takes center stage in the narrative. This shift in emphasis presumably explains the difference between the two accounts in their descriptions of the creative acts: in the second, plants and animals are created after humans, rather than before. But although the second account focuses on the creation of humans, this theme is by no means neglected in the first account. In fact, by means of quite different expressions and images, the two passages teach us about the nature of humanity.

First, humans have much in common with the rest of creation; they are created beings like those around them. The first creation account situates them inside the created order; human beings do not precede any part of creation but come into existence on the sixth day. When the second account describes the man being formed with his dual nature—body and soul—it deliberately avoids the term "spirit," which might have been understood as implying that a so-called divine spark had been incarnated in the body made from the ground. Instead, the text speaks of the "breath of life" that God imparts to man, but this breath is not itself divine (Genesis 2:7). The rest of the Scriptures confirm the wholly created nature of human beings. The prophet Zechariah (12:1) affirms this in particular with respect to the human spirit: "The oracle of the LORD, who stretched out the heavens and founded the earth, and formed the spirit of man within him."

On this point the biblical worldview differs from many rival understandings of humanity. For example, in *Atrahasis*, humans originate from a mixture of divine flesh and clay from the ground. Without resorting to such strong images, other worldviews have also considered the soul as being linked to the divine. Many Greek philosophers believed the soul to be eternal and immortal, belonging to the ideal world of immaterial realities. Its time in the body was only transitory and was meant to prepare it for its return to the spiritual world. Similar ideas continue to this day; we find them, for example, in the nebulous teachings of "New Age" spirituality. According to the Bible, however, humans are created in the totality of their being. This doctrine puts humans back in their place as created beings: they should not—and cannot—contend with God, who alone is eternal. Human beings do not in themselves possess immortality. Although in their state of original innocence they escaped death, this was only because of their ongoing access to the tree of life (Genesis 2:16; 3:22). Moreover, human beings, as "earthlings," have a vocation to live out in this world: we are called to have dominion over the earth (Genesis 1:28), and to cultivate the ground (Genesis 2:5, 15). While it is true that we humans should not focus solely on physical realities but lift up our eyes to our Creator, that doesn't mean that we originated in the invisible realm. Humans are not angels, let alone gods, but inhabitants of the earth, and thus an integral part of the visible, created universe.

What could seem, at first glance, to be demeaning for humanity, actually turns out to be a liberating message. If all people contain a divine spark, does it not inevitably follow that our present miserable condition is a consequence of our mixed nature? Is it not absurd that a divine element should find itself trapped inside a physical body? Since it is evident that humanity is so far from what it should be, it is only natural to wonder if the reason for our misfortune is found in the link between the spirit and the body: the spirit, misplaced in the material world, needs to be freed from it. In this conception, salvation necessarily implies the separation of the soul and the body: true happiness would be a state where we are no longer both spiritual and physical—which paradoxically amounts to the quest for a final condition where human beings would no longer be truly human.

The Genesis accounts in no way support this kind of dualistic view. Certainly, the Bible does not avoid the reality of human wretchedness: the explanation of our tragic condition is the central theme of the next part of the story (Genesis 3). But the tragedy is not a result of the way humanity came into existence; the disaster happens in *history*, when the man and the woman rebel against God's commandment. The problem is therefore not found in the make-up of human nature; it is not metaphysical, but moral. To attain salvation, human beings do not have to try and escape their own condition: there is no need to free the immortal soul from the material body. On the contrary, salvation, according to the Bible, is first and foremost the restoration of humans in all that we are, in accordance with God's initial plan. Jesus Christ is the embodiment of the true Human. In him we recover our humanity: Christians have "put on the new man who is continually being

renewed, for the sake of knowledge, in the image of his Creator"
(Colossians 3:10). It is therefore only logical that final salvation includes the resurrection of the physical body: complete
humans, body and soul, will participate in the new creation.

While humans are part of the created order, the creation
narrative particularly emphasizes what they have in common
with the animals. Many overlook that there is no separate
day for the creation of humans in the creation week; they
are created on the sixth day, as are the land animals. Part
of the commandment they receive is simply a reiteration
of God's earlier blessing on the sea creatures and birds: "Be
fruitful and multiply and fill the earth" (Genesis 1:22, 28).
The second account has the same method of creation used
for humans and animals: both are formed from the ground
(Genesis 2:7, 19).

But although human beings share much with the rest of
creation, especially the animals, they are also unique creatures.
Genetic studies have revealed the astonishing similarity of
the human genome to that of the great apes. Nevertheless,
man is not a "clothed apes." As proof, we need only imagine
for a moment what would happen if we tried to explain to a
friendly ape that we humans see ourselves as one of them. Even
the most well-educated chimpanzee, one who was used to
human company, would have difficulty following our reasoning! Recognizing this obvious truth by no means invalidates
the research that has identified similarities between humans

and animals. But minor genetic differences can have major consequences. Moreover, we should not reduce human beings to their genome—the uniqueness of human behavior, compared to other primates, shows how inadequate a "genes-only" approach is.

As much as Genesis affirms humanity's solidarity with the rest of creation, it also (and perhaps to a greater extent) emphasizes our unique nature. Once again, the two accounts support one another in teaching this truth, even if they express it in different ways. The first story uses the verb "to create" to describe the how humans come into existence. This verb is used sparingly in the chapter; it is only seen at key turning points in God's work of creation: at the very beginning, then when the first animals are made, and finally with man and woman. For the latter, it is even repeated three times to underscore the novelty of the event (Genesis 1:1, 21, 27). Only for the human race does the narrative explicitly mention the creation of the two sexes, even though the blessing given to the animals, calling them to multiply, implies they have been given reproductive organs. Humanity alone receives the order to have dominion over the earth. Special mention is made of the animals in this regard: "Subdue the earth and have dominion over the fish of the sea, the birds of the air and every beast that moves upon the earth" (Genesis 1:28). Although this re-emphasizes the link between humans and the animal kingdom, it becomes clear that this relationship is not symmetrical. While

these different elements combine to highlight the uniqueness
of human beings, the first account's teaching of the subject
converges in the declaration that human beings are created
"as the image of God."[24]

This expression has been the object of multiple interpretations over the course of history. It is clear that it refers to a particular privilege given to humanity, but opinions have differed
as to the nature of this privilege. The concept of the image
of God has often been associated with human beings' rational and moral abilities, and at times also with their original
innocence. John Calvin believed it comprised everything that
elevates humanity, in its creaturely state, above the animals:
original uprightness of mind, well-regulated emotions, intellectual abilities, and even our upright posture.[25] Others have
tried, on the contrary, to minimize the scope of the expression, to the point of seeing it merely as the privilege of having
dominion over the rest of creation. Today there is a fairly
broad consensus around a relational interpretation: humans
are the image of God, not primarily in particular aspects of
their nature; they as whole persons participate in their vocation to live in relationship with the Creator. We arrive at this
understanding of the *imago Dei* once we we realize that the
image only receives its value and dignity from its relationship with the original. The reason many refugees choose to
carry a few photographs in their meager luggage is not because
of their aesthetic value, and even less because of the paper

on which they are printed. They are precious because of the people they represent. In the same way,

> At that time, I say, when he had been advanced to the highest degree of honor, Scripture attributed nothing else to him than that he had been created in the image of God [Gen. 1:27], thus suggesting that man was blessed, not because of his own good actions, but by participation in God.[26]

Thus, human beings can only be understood in relation to God. Indeed, they cannot fulfill their true nature and develop their full potential unless they live in communion with the One whose image they are. Certainly, the qualitative differences between human beings and the rest of creation gives us a special status. But our true dignity comes only from our relationship with our Creator. Atheistic humanism thus proves to be illusory, despite its best intentions. This is not to deny that such an attitude can lead to remarkable achievements. But from the perspective of Genesis, such achievements never do justice to all that human beings are, for it is impossible to be human, in the full sense of the term, without relating to God.

When we accept this relational interpretation of the *imago Dei*, it brings us back to several of the traditional themes already mentioned which follow as corollaries of being God's image. In order to live in relationship with God, humans must possess rational and moral faculties. Since God is holy, men and women can only be in fellowship with him if they are completely innocent of sin. The privilege of dominion over the earth belongs to those who are the image of God; in this sense, they are God's representatives for and in the world.

Genesis 1 affirms that all humans enjoy the privilege of being the image of God. This egalitarian statement may have a polemical edge, as in the ancient Near East it was customary for those in power to declare themselves the sole representatives of the divine. Over against all forms of social, racial, or sexual discrimination, the text of Genesis insists that every human is created as the image of God. Thus, all share the same vocation: to live in relationship with their Creator and to represent him on earth. Likewise, they all deserve respect. Does not Jesus remind us that the commandment to love one's neighbor is "like" the commandment to love God (Matthew 22:39), since human beings' dignity derives from their Creator?

Genesis 2 develops the same theme of humanity's unique status. While the setting is more picturesque, in keeping with the text's literary genre, it points us in the same direction as the first account. Subduing the earth is expressed here by the instruction to keep and cultivate the garden. Dominion over the animals allows the man to name them—the prototype of scientific activity—but he does not find an equal among them. The differentiation of the two sexes of the human race also receives particular attention. Their moral responsibility is seen by the fact that the man and the woman receive a divine commandment. The privilege of being the image of God is particularly reflected in the duality of human nature: only humans are given the "breath of life" in addition to their corporal substance. Admittedly, the human body is not that of an animal; it too is fully human. Genetics has forever laid to rest the myth that humans retrace the evolutionary history of humankind in their embryonic development: from the very first moments of our existence, we grow as humans with our own genetic inheritance. Recent advances in neuroscience have also highlighted the way the human body, and in particular the brain, has adapted to the mind: even higher functions, like cognition, linguistic abilities, and spiritual awareness, are rooted in bodily reality, one that is specifically human.

In addition, the fact that humans cannot be reduced to their material dimension corresponds perfectly to their status as the image of God: "If mankind is the image of a Creator who is really distinct from the world, it is fitting that his being is really distinct from the visible realm of which he too is a part,"[27] which implies the duality of the human body and soul, one visible, the other invisible. Duality does not mean dualism, though: *both* parts of human nature are created by God. Moreover, "it is in the visible world that God wants his image,"[28] which implies the unity of human nature. Thus, the beginning of Genesis gives us a harmonious picture of what it is to be human: we are in solidarity with creation, while having the privilege of being the image of God. We are part of the visible creation, and yet transcend it. But above all, human beings are the result of the Creator's deliberate plan: they are not an accident of history, lost in the unblinking vastness of a hostile universe. No, God purposefully resolved to create us: "Let us make man in our image" (Genesis 1:26). The second creation account even shows God working with his hands to form the first man. As a result, we can be sure that God wants us to exist, and so trustingly commit ourselves to the plan that our Creator has wrought for humanity.

V

ENTERING INTO
GOD'S BLESSING

◆

V

IGHT FROM THE START, HUMAN existence is marked by God's blessing". The first chapter of Genesis, immediately after the creation of human beings "as the image of God," ends with the promise of the good things that God has allotted to them. Although God's declaration is largely phrased as a commandment, the text is explicit: this calling is a gift—"God blessed them and said to them" (Genesis 1:28). God had already blessed the first animals after creating them.

Animate beings have greater capacity for independent action than other created things, due to their mobility and their more advanced sensory and cognitive abilities. God's seal of approval on their existence shows that their greater independence is what the Creator wanted. It is not a stolen, runaway freedom that seeks to escape the creative order; it is a space for life granted by the Lord, the context in which living beings can use their faculties and flourish.

The account emphasizes three aspects of the blessing given to humanity: procreation, work, and food. Since these touch on fundamental elements of the human condition, we will look at each in more detail.

"BE FRUITFUL AND MULTIPLY AND FILL THE EARTH" (Genesis 1:28). Right from the beginning, the Creator gives a resounding "yes" to life. In the Bible, children are a gift from the Lord, a gift we are called to receive with gratitude. The difficulties of pension systems in the developed world are a stark reminder of the importance of being receptive to new life—an attitude that is both a command and a blessing from God. Of course, this does not mean wanting children just so that they can foot the bill for our retirement. Nevertheless, demographic changes in the West are evidence that a society dies (both literally and figuratively) when it refuses to accept the human calling of procreation.

The term "procreation" merits a closer look. Its etymology communicates the dignity that parents have: they are participating in the Lord's creative work. Their union allows a new *person* to come into being. Every time conception occurs, we behold a mystery: the tiny being that has just begun their life journey is not an extension of their parents; he or she is an individual, with his or her own unique character, heritage, and story. Like his or her father and mother, he or she is also created "in the image of God" and endowed with an inalienable dignity. The first birth recorded in the Bible communicates this sense of wonder that still grips us when we consider the privilege (and also responsibility) that God has entrusted to human beings. Cain's name is related to the verb *qānâ*, "to procreate"; for Eve says, "I have procreated a man, with the help of the LORD" (Genesis 4:1).

The first blessing bestowed on humanity shows that procreation, and with it, sexuality, is part of the Creator's original plan. It is important to emphasize this teaching from the opening chapters of Genesis, because a certain tradition—whose influence is still felt today—associated sexual reproduction with sin. Thus, St. Augustine considered that it was the sexual desire that accompanies intercourse, even within marriage, that was responsible for original sin being transmitted to the child. A widespread feeling that sexuality is something dirty has persisted to this day. This understanding of sexuality is no doubt supported by the perversions that are regrettably associated with it. However, it is essential to distinguish between the gift of sexuality, part of God's will, and the ways it has been abused because of human sinfulness. The Bible does not idealize asceticism; the apostle Paul prefers celibacy to marriage, not because of any supposed purity linked to virginity, but because it means one is more available to serve (1 Corinthians 7:26). Sexuality is part of the Creator's plan, and "everything God has created is good, and nothing is to be rejected if it is taken with thanksgiving" (1 Timothy 4:4).

Although Genesis 1 places procreation at the head of God's blessing to humankind, it also warns us against certain deviations in the way sexuality is used. Admittedly, we should not reduce sexual union to the role of procreation: the second creation account presents it as the seal confirming the marital bond between a man and a woman, without any mention of the children who might be born as a result: "A man shall leave his father and mother and be joined to his wife, and the two shall become one flesh" (Genesis 2:24). But the Creator's "yes" to life reveals how precarious it would be to use one's sexuality solely for personal satisfaction with no intention of starting a family. This does not exclude birth control: we are called to manage our reproductive ability—as with all our faculties—with responsibility and intelligence. It would be a mistake to interpret "be fruitful and multiply" as an obligation to have as many children as possible. Since human beings are created in God's image, we have a certain amount of freedom that we must manage wisely. Accordingly, couples are called to think carefully about their life plans and the circumstances that are conducive to raising a child.

Although the calling to have children will be answered by each couple in their own way, taking into account their particular circumstances, that does not mean they should intentionally opt out of God's blessing.

When we read the blessing that God announces upon the creation of human beings, we are inevitably reminded that we live in a world where sin has disrupted creation's good order. Only when we compare this with God's original plan can we fully appreciate how much suffering results from deviations from the created order. These deviations can be the consequence of our own decision, of someone else's sin, or of illness: they bring their share of pain quite simply because they are in tension with creation's design. Without wanting to equate the various situations and different causes involved in the inability to procreate, God's blessing on humanity shows childlessness to be a privation that is legitimately painful. While infertility is a difficult ordeal for any couple, abortion is a genuine tragedy, one often undertaken in the greatest secrecy. We might also point out that the calling to be fruitful is addressed to a humanity created with sexual differentiation—"male and female" as the passage says (Genesis 1:27). "In those slightly crazy years, when dads weren't in fashion any more, she made a baby all by herself," sang Jean-Jacques Goldman.[29] The fact that a child can only be born from the union of a man and a woman is not just a biological fact. A child needs a father and a mother—both to come into existence *and* to develop.

Anyone who has had to bring up a child on their own knows just how impossible it is to combine the roles of mother and father. Here again, straying from the Creator's intention (be it deliberately or, more often, unwillingly) carries a high price. How precious it is to remember that God is "a father to the fatherless and a defender of widows" (Psalm 68:5); his grace can give single parents the strength they need to cope with their responsibilities.

THE SECOND PART OF GOD'S command-plus-blessing to humankind concerns dominion over the earth: "Subdue it, and have dominion over the fish of the sea and over the birds of the air and over every living thing that moves on the earth" (Genesis 1:28). As humans are the image of God in their relationship with the Creator—we could say "for God" — they are also the image of God for the world. Through humans' rule over the rest of creation, they express their dignity as God's image; vicariously, men and women are the Creator's representatives on earth. This special status provides the basis not only for agriculture and craftsmanship, but also for science, technology, and the arts. Human beings fulfill their vocation to have dominion over the earth by using their manual and rational faculties to expand their knowledge of natural laws, increase their mastery of creation's structures, and shape their environment. We can therefore admire the work of skilled craftspeople, scientific and technical achievements, or great works of art, as different fulfillments of humanity's creative vocation. It is not insignificant that in English, the word "profession" means both the public declaration of one's faith and the job that one does. Far from being merely a way of paying the bills, work is part of the blessing that the Creator bestows on humanity—a blessing that is both a mission and a privilege. Once again, thinking about God's plan for creation helps us to understand the misfortune of those who are prevented from carrying it out: unemployment is not just a material problem; it degrades the dignity of human beings who find themselves unable to use their abilities to work.

The portrait of humans' original situation that we see in Scripture is markedly different from popular representations of paradise: nowhere do we find the "noble savage" who receives everything from nature in total passivity. From the beginning, humans are civilized beings who shape their environment and leave their mark on it. The verbs used in Genesis 1 to describe human activity express the active exercise of authority. The first one in particular, which we translate "to subdue," often conveys the idea of violence: it is used for military victory over enemies (Numbers 32:29), the act of enslaving someone (Jeremiah 34:11), and rape (Esther 7:8). When we read the divine blessing in the light of Genesis 2, we understand that this is not meant to be a tyrannical reign: dominion over the earth finds its expression in the human's call to cultivate (literally "serve") and keep the garden (Genesis 2:15). However, the second creation narrative also shows us an earth that, in its initial state, is hardly fit for people to live on. Although the necessary elements are already in place (workable soil, and water), cultivation is required for them to produce fruit. It is true that what follows shows us that human rebellion has made the work difficult: the ground now bears thorns and thistles (Genesis 3:17–19). But even before the fall, Adam and Eve had work to do: they cultivated the garden. By shaping their environment, humans are simply fulfilling their creational vocation. They continue the work of God himself who prepared a beautiful orchard as a habitat for human beings. The Bible in no way endorses distrust of the techniques of civilization, skilled craftsmanship, or scientific endeavor. Humanity is not a mere part of nature, living in symbiosis with it. Nor are humans slaves of a deified natural order. Human beings transcend the rest of creation; they are called to have dominion over the earth and the animals. They therefore have the freedom, indeed the vocation, to modify their environment in order to create a favorable habitat for themselves. The garden of Eden is neither a virgin forest nor is it Cockaigne, the mythical land of plenty.

If it is as God's representatives that human beings exercise dominion over the earth, then the nature of that reign becomes clearer. On the one hand, it expresses a genuine dignity, (dare we say it!) a superiority of humanity. Even as we consider the ways that human activity threatens the delicate balance of the earth's ecosystems, we must not forget that the conservation of nature is not the supreme value. On the other hand, human dominion over the rest of creation must image God's reign over his creation—and it is thereby obvious that believers cannot avoid their responsibility for the environment. God's governance is the complete opposite of what so often characterizes the approach fallen human beings take to nature, namely exploitation. God cares for his creation; he provides it with what it needs to develop and fulfill its true potential. Human beings are thus called, in their own limited way, to imitate the Creator. One may have heard the poignant saying, "We do not inherit the earth from our ancestors; we borrow it from our children." The notion of creation puts things in ever greater perspective: we are not only accountable to our children, but to God. It is from the Creator that we have received this earth; it is to him that we will have to give an account for the state in which we pass it to the next generation.

This broader perspective also allows for a more nuanced view of technology, as we have already outlined. If mastery of nature is part of humanity's original vocation, then technical skill, like all human works, has since the fall become ambiguous. It can either be an expression of the freedom that we, beings created in God's image, have with respect to nature, or it can be born of our desire to rise above our place as created beings. Humans in rebellion against their Creator proclaim themselves at the same time enemies of creation. Instead of looking after creation, they are tempted to exploit nature. Instead of having dominion over the earth as wise stewards, they often seek to arbitrarily change natural structures to their liking. Yet discernment is not an easy matter, for where do we draw the line between the work of civilization that humans need to do and an abusive transformation? We have difficulty even imagining the reluctance of some of our predecessors to adopt street lighting when it was first introduced in towns and cities, blurring the natural rhythm of day and night. The mad cow disease scandal, where cows who were fed meat developed an illness contagious to humans, reminded us that human beings cannot disdain the natural order (in which cows do not eat meat) without suffering the consequences. Is it dominion over the earth, which brings out the full potential of nature and ensures the survival of humanity? Or tyranny? The hard task of evaluation cannot be avoided, and only the tangible results of this appraisal will prove, with hindsight, to be conclusive.

THE BLESSING THAT GOD SPEAKS concerning humanity concludes with a third fundamental aspect of the human condition: the need for food. The challenge of providing for this need determines to a large extent the daily activities of a significant part of the world's population. But scarcity is not the only situation in which food becomes a central concern:

one need only survey the range of magazines on cooking, health, or women's lifestyle, to realize that the question of what we eat is ever-present, even in societies where food is plentiful. Although the subject of food is rarely addressed in Christian teaching today, the opposite is true of the Bible: fully aware of the critical role that eating plays in human life, the Scriptures address this theme over and over. We read of the extraordinary provision of food in the form of manna during the Exodus, and again with Jesus's feeding of the five thousand; the dietary prescriptions in the law of Moses; the apostle Paul's denunciation of orgies; the choice of a meal as a sacrament of both the old and new covenants (the Passover meal and the Lord's Supper)—the subject of food appears many times in the Bible. It is thus fitting that the Genesis accounts give pride of place to the theme of eating, and no coincidence that the first sin is described as one of consumption: eating the fruit of the tree of the knowledge of good and evil (Genesis 3:6).

In the blessing from the first creation account, we see that God is concerned with humankind's nutritional needs: "Behold, I give you every plant yielding seed that is found on all the earth, and every fruit tree that yields seed; it shall be your food" (Genesis 1:29).

The contrast with the Mesopotamian epic *Atrahasis* could not be sharper.[32] In the latter, as we have already seen, the gods create humans to do their work for them. In Genesis, on the

◆ ◆ ◆

The tree of the knowledge of good and evil

In popular culture, the forbidden fruit has long been represented as an apple. The reason for this is found in a Latin play on words: "evil" and "apple" are both *malum*. Although we find the tree of life in other, non-biblical texts from the same period, no parallel exists in ancient Near Eastern literature for the garden of Eden's second central tree. It is true that we find trees of knowledge or wisdom—which are, therefore, also trees of life—but there is no tree of knowledge *of good and evil* as distinct from the tree of life.[30] What is meant by the knowledge of good and evil that human beings acquired when they ate from this tree?

We may reject several interpretations: it cannot be knowledge in general; this was not withheld from humanity before the fall. Nor did humans discover in that moment the distinction between good and evil; the commandment that God had given them already contained a clear indication of the difference between good and evil. Could it be that humanity now knows evil from personal experience? But the Genesis text makes it clear that God himself has the knowledge of good and evil: "Behold, the man has become like one of us," said the LORD God, "concerning the knowledge of good and evil" (Genesis 3:22). God does not know evil from experience. Omniscience is a possible interpretation: humans wanted to take this divine prerogative for themselves. But in this case, we are obliged to understand the remark that fallen humanity now possesses the knowledge of good and evil as purely ironic. For, obviously, humans have not become omniscient.

The most likely interpretation is that the knowledge of good and evil means independence in moral choices: the will to decide for oneself what is good and what is evil, rather than receiving this definition from another. This meaning makes sense in the passages that use corresponding expressions: children do not know good and evil, in the sense that they receive ethical rules from their parents and those around them, not yet reflecting critically on them (even though they are already perfectly aware of the difference between what is permitted and what is forbidden; Deuteronomy 1:39; Isaiah 7:15–16). The king knows good and evil, in the sense that in ancient societies he is both lawmaker and judge (2 Samuel 14:17; 1 Kings 3:9). The tree of the knowledge of good and evil was forbidden to human beings, since their duty was to receive God's moral criteria. Highly esteemed commentators have supported this interpretation, including the Reformer John Calvin, the neo-orthodox theologian Karl Barth, the Catholic Bible scholar Roland de Vaux, and the Protestant philosopher Paul Ricœur.[31]

◆ ◆ ◆

contrary, God takes care of humans and provides for their needs. The fact that human beings are dependent on divine care reminds us of our created status: we did not come into being by ourselves, and our life still depends on God's providence. Thus it is possible to see our need for food as a symbol of the creational dependence that characterizes humanity. The fact we need to eat regularly is a physical embodiment of our true status: we depend on something outside of ourselves in order to go on living.

Like all other consequences of being created, the need for food is not a constraint for humankind. Quite the opposite; it is a source of joy, as long as it is experienced in the harmony meant to characterize creation. In the first two chapters of Genesis, there is no sign of any difficulty in obtaining life's necessities; the context for human existence is marked only by the Creator's generosity. The first upset occurs when the man and the woman usurp the right to decide what they will eat, and take from the tree of the knowledge of good and evil; as a result, it becomes difficult, even impossible at times, to find daily bread: "Cursed shall be the earth because of you; with difficulty shall you eat of it all the days of your life. It shall bring forth for you thorns and thistles, and you shall eat the plants of the field. By the sweat of your brow you shall eat bread" (Genesis 3:17–19). However, even after the fall, the goodness of creaturely dependence that food symbolizes is not nullified. The Preacher insists that the pleasures of a frugal but well-made meal are a precious gift from the Creator: "Go, eat your bread with joy, and drink your wine with a merry heart, for God has already approved what you do" (Ecclesiastes 9:7). As well as the enjoyment it can bring, eating eating grants humans an openness to the exterior they cannot live without: the body is not a closed system; it continuously assimilates and rejects physical matter. This arrangement, which allows toxic substances to be eliminated, is also essential for the growth and regeneration of the body's living tissue.

What holds for the physical body is also true relationally: human beings cannot thrive in isolation. Humankind is social in nature; meeting other people is essential for life. It is therefore noteworthy that meals have been opportune moments for fellowship ever since biblical times. Similarly, eating can become a symbol of openness to the divine. We have already mentioned the sacrament of the Lord's Supper. More generally, receiving God's word, so crucial for salvation, is comparable to our need for nourishment. As Moses reminds the people of Israel after they have crossed of the desert: "[The LORD your God] let you hunger and gave you manna to eat, which you did not know and which your fathers did not know, so that you might learn that man does not live by bread alone, but lives by all that comes from the mouth of the LORD" (Deuteronomy 8:3).

Once we grasp its symbolic importance, we can understand why eating is not just a simple biological necessity. On the contrary, it is intimately linked to the emotional and spiritual dimensions of the human person, such that problems encountered in one of these areas will have an impact on the others. Bad news takes away our appetite; more seriously, anorexia and bulimia have deeper causes than poor eating habits. The destructive work of sin shows itself in the issue of eating as in other areas of human life. The consequences are felt in the lives of individuals and societies: the imbalance between excess for some and scarcity, even famine, for others, is nauseating.

When we consider these eating disorders—both individual and societal—the blessing that the Creator announces is strikingly ordered. The narrative suggests that plant life, which arose on the third day, can be divided into three categories: green plants (like grass), plants yielding seed (such as cereals), and fruit trees. The plants in the first group are given as food to the animals; those of the last two groups, to humans (Genesis 1:11–12, 29–30). When we add to this human dominion over the animals, an orderly structure emerges in which the different kinds of living things each have their place and relate to each other. What a striking contrast to the suffering that eating disorders cause in today's world! At this point, the creation account serves as a warning, a stern "call to order," urging us to recover, if only in some small way, the harmony that God intended at the outset. As Creator, God cares about every aspect of our existence. The relevance of his word is not limited to the "spiritual" domain, while our everyday lives remain untouched. Quite the opposite: everything in life becomes an expression of faith. As the apostle Paul reminds the Christians in Corinth: "Whether you eat or drink, or whatever you do, do it all to the glory of God" (1 Corinthians 10:31).

◆ ◆ ◆

Were humans vegetarian before the fall?

The Genesis accounts do not mention animal-based food. Only after the flood does the Bible talk of eating animals (Genesis 9:3). Should we conclude from this that humans—and indeed all animals—were vegetarian before the fall?

One might initially be tempted to answer in the affirmative, especially since the vegetarian diet of the ferocious beasts is used as an image to describe the perfect peace that characterizes the eschatological kingdom: "The wolf shall dwell with the lamb; the leopard shall lie down with the kid. ... The lion shall eat fodder like the ox" (Isaiah 11:6, 7; cf. 65:25). The law of "eat or be eaten" hardly seems to match the harmony of a creation as yet unspoiled by sin.

A word of caution, however: it is always risky to construct a theory on what the text does not say. Although there is no mention in Genesis of animal-based food before the flood, nowhere is meat-eating explicitly prohibited. Adam's son Abel, a shepherd, offered animal sacrifices: it is possible that he also fed himself from his flock (Genesis 4:2, 4). Genesis does not mention a change in diet as being one of the consequences of the fall. Even after the first human couple's rebellion, the text only refers to the cultivation of the soil, which will now produce not just useful or edible plants, but also thorns and thistles (Genesis 3:18). Even if this remark suggests that changes have occurred in the natural world, we must beware of unbridled speculation: positing that all the food chains in the animal kingdom only began at this point would imply, in reality, a new creative act, which would take place after the first sin. The mutual dependencies between predators and prey are too subtle and diverse to be the result of the disruption of the order laid down at creation, caused by humanity's sin. The animal kingdom, including the balance of power between different species, bears the marks of creative ingenuity. Thus, we can understand why God, in the book of Job, takes delight in powerful, savage beasts: they reflect, in the very fear that they inspire, the Creator's great power. To give but one example, in a highly poetic passage, God marvels at the crocodile's jaws that inspire terror (Job 41:14; cf. 38:39 for the lion; 39:27–30 for the eagle).

Certainly, predation *appears* cruel to us. But is this not the result of projecting human categories? It is not so obvious that animal death, even when caused by another creature, is a *moral* evil, one that is unworthy of the first creation.

Why do the Genesis creation accounts not mention meat-eating? To answer this question, let us remember that they are not treatises on zoology. It is therefore not a problem that their presentation of the living creatures is schematic. The arrangements made concerning food must express the *order* of the created world: the different categories of living beings relate to each other and depend on each other—human beings, birds, land and sea animals, the different kinds of plants. The story mentions, for humans, both dominion over the animals and plant-based food. It is therefore possible that humans were also allowed to take animals for food.

◆　◆　◆

VI

OBEYING GOD'S COMMANDMENT

◆

VI

*T*HE BLESSING THAT GOD ANNOUNCES to humanity in Genesis 1 corresponds to the commandment that he addresses to Adam in Genesis 2: "Of all the trees of the garden you shall eat freely. But of the tree of the knowledge of good and evil, you shall not eat. For the day that you eat of it, you will surely die" (Genesis 2:16–17). In fact, blessing and commandment go hand in hand: from the beginning, human existence is marked by God's kindness *and* is lived out within the boundaries provided by the law. Moreover, the blessing of the first creation account is, to a large extent, expressed as an order; to receive the blessing, humans must observe it and put their vocation into practice. In the same way, the commandment given in the second account defines the environment in which humans will live; therefore, it is as much favor from God as it is the privilege of a responsibility conferred.

The initial commandment is dual in nature: it has two sides, one positive and the other negative. Too often, people only remember the second part, the prohibition. But it is the two elements together that constitute the Creator's revealed will for humanity. They use exactly the same grammatical form, as if to emphasize the close link between them. In Hebrew, to give additional force to a verb, the infinitive is added before the conjugated form. Literally, the original text reads: "Of all the trees of the garden, TO EAT you shall eat. But of the tree of the knowledge of good and evil, you shall not eat. For the day that you eat of it, TO DIE you shall die." The fact that the first command uses this emphatic form clearly emphasizes the importance of the positive side of the commandment. Far from being limited to prohibitions that restrict human freedom, the law actually does the opposite, granting pleasure. Enjoying the good gifts of creation is a divine *order*!

One question arises, however: Why is this invitation to take pleasure necessary? Don't human beings naturally make the most of the good fruits that creation gives them? Do we really need an explicit divine commandment to do that? The way the Genesis account is worded suggests that humans, left to their own devices, are unable to enjoy the blessings of creation. Indeed, we see to our dismay that it is not that easy to genuinely enjoy the good things in life. Not only do human beings err in what they associate with pleasure (and this can go as far as the perversion of masochism), but more subtly, the pursuit of wholesome pleasures can end up becoming a means of selfishly satisfying our own desires, while disregarding, or even exploiting, other people. The opposite mistake is also possible: in order to avoid excesses and the misuse of good things, some choose asceticism, thereby shutting themselves off from the enjoyment of creation that God wants humans to experience.

The negative side of the first commandment shows that humans need to receive from their Creator the instructions necessary for true pleasure. When Eve ignores the prohibition, she does so precisely because she sees that the forbidden fruit is "good for food and pleasing to the eye" (Genesis 3:6). This is no surprise: it is part of the good and perfect creation, which comes from Lord's hand. However, the rest of the story tragically shows that human beings cannot decide for themselves how to enjoy it; in order to avoid disaster, they must receive the rules of the game from the One who invented them.

The fact that humans are placed under God's law right from the start corresponds to their position as created beings. Humanity is always in second place with respect to the

Creator; this is why we must receive the definitions of what is good or evil from the One who is superior to us. Humans cannot decide for themselves the rules that should govern their behavior. The conception of freedom that results is almost diametrically opposed to the contemporary definition: for created beings, freedom is not the same as independence; it does not mean making autonomous decisions about choices and conduct. On the contrary, humans are only truly free when they accept God's law. They do not exist in a moral vacuum that offers them various options of equal value. Rather, humans are always already situated under the divine order, engaged in a covenant relationship with the Creator. The freedom of the one who is committed "for better or for worse" is not to break that commitment, but to live it out fully within the agreed framework. Disregarding a commitment always constitutes a rebellion, a betrayal.

The covenant in which human beings are situated by creation may at first seem like a restriction. But as the rest of the Genesis account shows, it is suicidal to think that freedom lies in breaking the rules. Right from the first prohibition, which restricts the choice of trees they are allowed to eat from, humans only find their satisfaction and fulfillment when they obey God's law and gladly accept the status of created beings. As soon as they overstep their bounds, to break free from the Creator's commandment, they set foot on the road to ruin. We cannot exist outside of the place that has been assigned to us by the act of creation. The fish who wants to leave the water, to be more free, will not live very long. Accepting the limits associated with the status of created beings is the only possible position for humans. As Ecclesiastes 12:13 puts it:

> Fear God, and keep his commandments;
> for this is the whole of man.

It is therefore crucial to rediscover the biblical theme of the fear of God, which is so absent from contemporary spirituality, at least in the West. Admittedly, one must distinguish a child's respect for their parent from a servile dread that makes relationship impossible. But while it is true that we can only exist within the framework defined by God for human life, there is nothing worse for us than disobeying the law. What consideration could justify our departure from God's will? To give an example from my family history: my grandmother, like many women of her generation, was left after World War II without any news of her husband, who was a soldier. She had to live without him, yet she had no certain proof that he was dead. She was thirty-eight years old at the end of the war. When opportunities for remarrying arose, she always held that the vows made on her wedding day were binding until she knew for sure that her partner had lost his life. As far as I know, her faithfulness to the commitment she made and to God's law seemed completely normal to her, undeserving of any particular merit. Her attitude is a telling example of the priority given to obedience—an attitude that, in her case, was rewarded in living out her old age surrounded by an affectionate family.

If my evaluation of current Christian practice is correct, we urgently need to relearn how to make God's commandments central to the ethical choices we face. Reading Christian works from the past and meeting believers from other cultures can help us take to heart the biblical theme of the fear of the Lord. It may also be useful to ponder the causes that have led to the devaluing of submission, obedience, and respect for authority, which were until relatively recent times held in high esteem. We will then be better armed to resist their influence. It is probable, however, that these causes include abuses of power, so our consideration must also alert us to wrong understandings of obedience. Granted, it is not possible to fully analyze the many complex factors that have contributed to our current situation. And yet, I believe it is possible to identify three major factors.

The first, in my opinion, is the trauma inflicted by totalitarian regimes—both fascist and communist—with their demand for total, blind obedience. The Nazi slogan "*Führer befiehl, wir folgen*" ("Führer, give your orders, we will follow") led to unspeakable crimes. Those who, for a time, had to live under this kind of rule are rightly mistrustful of any authority that demands their total allegiance. A second and more recent factor: we have witnessed first-hand a religious fanaticism in which murder is claimed to be obedience to divine law. The example of suicide bombers, who in God's name demonstrate complete submission to their ideology, cannot help but serve as a warning against misguided religious zeal.

These two factors can explain the mistrust we find today regarding any authority that demands submission and obedience. This mistrust is, first, beneficial; had it been acted on in the circumstances just mentioned, humanity would have been spared a great number of crimes. However, we must not forget that this observation does not in any way invalidate true fear of the Lord. It merely indicates, crucially, that obedience has no intrinsic virtue: it all depends to whom and to what we are submitting. It is certainly true that no *human* authority should ever demand blind obedience. But this restriction flows precisely from the fact that only God, as Creator, is entitled to our wholehearted love, just as the Shema, Israel's confession of faith, declares: "Listen, O Israel, the LORD is our God, the LORD is one. You shall love the LORD your God with all your heart, with all your soul, and with all your strength" (Deuteronomy 6:4–5). All people must acknowledge that they are equal before this one Lord; no one can declare themselves the master of others' consciences or lives.

The example of religious extremists willing to kill also shows us that claiming to act in God's name is not the same as truly serving him. We can never know God's will apart from the revelation of his law contained in his word. From the start, Adam, in the garden of Eden, needed to hear the word of God to get his bearings. This is even more true for us, ever since sin upset the created order and darkened our minds. Only the diligent study of the Scriptures can protect us from the danger of confusing our own ambitions with God's will. In fact, far from making us easy targets for fanaticism, studying the Bible, patiently and with hearts open to what God wants to say to us, is the best antidote against all human voices who abusively demand our obedience. Throughout church history, martyrs have shown by their lives that those who bow the knee to God can stand up to human powers. Ordinary villagers were able to resist the Nazi authorities, in Chambon-sur-Lignon, a Protestant stronghold of the French Haute-Loire region, to save the lives of some five thousand Jews. Their collective action is one of the finest examples of civic courage, one pro-duced by a faith grounded in Bible reading.

A third factor may explain a certain reticence toward the idea of submitting to the Word: the example of some of the believers of the past cautions us against a legalistic faith. Many do not wish to reproduce the example of spirituality character-ized by the observance of external rules. Here again, we must recognize that this reaction is justified, at least in part. Believers are called to enjoy the freedom of the children of God; it does not honor the Father to deny oneself the blessings of creation or to think that one can identify a "good Christian" by their old-fashioned way of dress or speech. Let us be careful, how-ever, not to seek a cure that is worse than the disease: license is no better than legalism! The requirement of complete submission to the word is right; the zeal of Christians who seem legalistic to us can even be an inspiration. It is not the willingness to obey God wholeheartedly that is questionable, but the flawed understanding of what genuinely pleases the Lord. The proper remedy is thus to go back to the Scriptures in order to correct and deepen our knowledge of God's will.

The Genesis account shows us what is at stake when we think about how to consider obedience to the divine commandment: this is not a question of personal taste, which might be left to the discretion of each individual, but a question of life and death. We must choose between the garden's two trees: on the one hand, respect for God's law and life within the framework defined by his word, which gives continuous access to the tree of life, the latter being a symbol of life-giving communion with the Creator. On the other hand, the autonomous choice of what is good and the rejection of the limits imposed by God's commandment. But in this case it is no longer possible to eat from the tree of life; outside of paradise, humans are left to their own devices and headed for death. This choice between life and death is one that each of us must make, as we see in Deuteronomy 30:15–18:

> See: I set before you today life and good, death and evil;
> I command you today to love the LORD your God, to
> walk in his ways and to keep his commandments, his

> laws and his judgments. Then you shall live. ... But if
> your heart turns away, if you do not listen ... I announce
> to you today that you will be totally destroyed; you will
> not live long.

Humanity's tragic history contains abundant proof that since the first human couple, each of us has chosen death, rather than life. In his grace—which goes beyond the creation covenant—God has set up yet another tree: at the cross, the Son of God suffered the death sentence in place of rebellious human beings. In this way he has reopened the way to the tree of life for all those who return to God, trusting in his grace and submitting anew to his law. The final book of the Bible communicates this salutary truth in figurative language that echoes the Genesis account: "Blessed are those who wash their robes [in the blood of the Lamb], so that they may have the right to the tree of life" (Revelation 22:14). The blood of the Lamb, signifying Christ's death, enables us to be purified of the uncleanness resulting from our rebellion. When we place our trust in Christ's redemptive work accomplished at the cross, we recover the right to enter paradise and to live in communion with our Creator, the source of all life.

VII

ACCEPTING
YOUR LIMITS

◆

VII

F ROM THE START, THE SCRIPTURES portray humans as finite beings, placed in a specific setting that their Creator prepared for them: "The LORD God took the man and set him in the garden of Delights to cultivate it and keep it" (Genesis 2:15). Admittedly, it is not easy to interpret the geographical indications given in the Eden story.[33] Nevertheless, in the narrative, paradise clearly appears as a specific place that God has made ready to accommodate the first humans. In this way, from creation onward, human beings have been localized. Far from being a bothersome constraint, this reality is a result of the Creator's concern for his creatures: what God prepares for them is a place of delights! Inhabiting a *place* is thus, for humankind, a blessing, and also the context for their vocation: humans are called to continue the loving care that the Creator has shown in his preparation of paradise. Right up to the last vision in the New Testament, the destiny of God's saved people is linked to a place: they do not just inhabit the new earth, but more precisely, the new Jerusalem (Revelation 21:1–22:5). In this way, the final state does not erase humankind's localization, because the latter was part of creation and therefore good, very good. The loss of a place is one of sin's damaging consequences. Cain's lament to God is typical of the wretchedness experienced by the sinner wandering far from paradise: "My fault is too heavy to bear. Behold, you drive me away today from the face of this earth, and from your face, I shall be hidden. I will be a fugitive and a wanderer on the earth, and whoever finds me will kill me" (Genesis 4:13–14).

Localization in space and time is a limitation for humans: we always exist in a given place and time, and we cannot be everywhere at once. We should not make the mistake of expecting technical progress to free us from the human condition: despite all the advances in transport and communication systems, we remain bound to a *single* location. Wanting to break free of it is a sign we have listened to the serpent's sly words, which long ago tempted the first humans to want to become like gods.

This limitation is manifested most tangibly in the fact that we live in bodies: the body is the place where each of us encounters our localization in space and time. Whereas our imagination is (nearly) limitless, our body anchors us in the material world where we are subject to the laws of physics and chemistry. It is quite remarkable: wherever we go, we get ourselves there in our body! As long as we live, we cannot exist anywhere other than in our body. Not only does our body oblige us to be in a particular place, it also has a specific shape: it is with a body of a certain height, with a certain beauty (or lack of), with a certain skin color, that I meet the world around me. The limits that result from embodied existence do not just concern the body; the latter simply happens to be the most tangible aspect of the human condition. Each person is born into a particular family, grows up in a country with its own history and culture, faces life with a unique set of skills and experiences, and sees the world through the lens of their individual character.

The Bible's origin accounts place particular emphasis on the sexual differentiation of humanity: human beings are male *or* female; there is no vagueness or mixture of the two. This distinction between individuals can be taken as symbolic of all other finitudes. It stands like a protective wall (one that, despite medical ingenuity, remains impenetrable) against the illusion that *my* experience could encompass that of humanity: I am unable to exist in the world other than as a woman *or* as a man. Even if (thank goodness!) there is an ongoing dialog between these two modes of existence, there is no way for me to see the other point of view from the inside. As a result, the distinction between the male and female reminds us human beings of our finitude, of our created state.

Since our finitude has been fixed since creation, we can accept it without regret. The biblical worldview refuses the idea that human beings' corporal, limited constitution is an imperfection; in particular, it is wrong to consider it the cause of our sinful nature. Quite the opposite: we can discern, in our finite existence, the location where the Lord wants to bless us and calls us to serve him—as we remember the garden of Delights. Therefore, the way we consider the limits of our human existence depends directly on our attitude to human-kind's status as created beings. If we accept the fact that human beings are created, we can understand all the specific facets of individuals as aspects that make them unique. Gratefully accepting our bodies, our family, our character, and so on, is part of the challenge to glorify and serve the Creator in the place he assigns to us. I don't have to be jealous of the greener grass on my neighbor's side of the fence because I am called to live in my place, not theirs.

Accepting our place as created beings does not, of course, mean denying the harmful consequences of sin: not all the limits that we find in our world are the result of creation. The constraints that are produced by disease, or by racial, economic, or educational discrimination, do not come from creation. We therefore have a duty to fight against them as hard as we can. But this battle will never be driven by the revolt against finitude itself (which in any case would be untenable), against the fact that each individual existence can only express a tiny fraction of the diversity of human experience and can never rival the divine fullness. By contrast, the person who acknowledges that they are a created being can, with joyful confidence, embrace the limits of their existence: these are a sign of their individuality and provide the framework within which God blesses the person he created and calls them to serve him. In this way, the Christian can resist the yearning for a life with no limits, the desire to live a hundred lives.

Human beings are not called to "live a hundred lives," but just one: the hope of eternal life has nothing to do with the (hopeless) desire to break free of all our limits, as described in Jean-Jacques Goldman's pop song. In Christian hope, the limit that is done away with is that posed by death—which was not part of God's good creation but entered later because of sin. Human finitude is not called into question: it is appointed for us to live just one life (Hebrews 9:27), and all the way into eternity we will exist as individuals—differentiated from other people and from our Creator.

Jean-Jacques Goldman's Vivre cent vies
(Live a Hundred Lives)

J'aimerais tant être au pluriel
Quand mon singulier me rogne les ailes
Être une star en restant anonyme
Vivre à la campagne mais en centre ville
Effacer mes solitudes
Sans Dieu ni famille, sans habitude
Blanche princesse, ou masseuse à Bangkok
Sage philosophe et puis chanteur de rock
Brûler mes nuits, noyer mes jours
Être fidèle à des milliers d'amours
Vivre sa vie, rien que sa vie
Crever d'envies, un petit tour et fini
Ça fait trop mal, c'est pas moral
Vivre même à demi, tant pis, mais vivre cent vies[34]

How I'd love to be plural
When being singular clips my wings
Be a pop star while remaining unknown
Live in the countryside, but downtown
Rub out my loneliness
No God or family, no habits
A white princess, or masseuse in Bangkok
Wise philosopher and then rock singer
Burn up my nights, drown my days
Be faithful to thousands of lovers
Living your own life, and nothing but your own life
So many desires, one little go and that's all
It's too painful, it's immoral
Live, even if just by half, never mind, but live a
    hundred lives.

◆ ◆ ◆

What might be considered as restrictive is, of course, the only condition in which humans, as created beings, can fully live. Does Goldman sense this, in some vague way, when he suggests that he would be happy with a hundred lives lived "by half"? Refusing our limits and rebelling against our finitude always carries a price: what we try to gain in quantity is lost in quality of life. The Jesuit theologian Hans Urs von Balthasar's remarks about love are valid for human experience in general: "The man who has a tranquil, monogamous marriage gets more knowledge of love than the debauchee who gives himself up to every sensual enjoyment"[35]—despite, or in fact because of, the restriction that is taken on.

Seen from this perspective, certain trends in Western societies should raise questions. It is not far-fetched to consider the remote control as a powerful metaphor for our mobility in this modern age: channel-hopping is not limited to our television habits; it also applies to many of the commitments that we make (or, more accurately, fail to make). Faithfulness has become a virtue in short supply, and we should ask ourselves, when looking for the cause of this change, whether the mad frenzy that seeks to embrace all possible experience is much to blame. Faithfulness in a given situation, whether it be at work, at church, or in marriage, necessarily implies that we give up other options. In particular, the "yes" that is declared on the wedding day requires thereafter saying "no" countless times, without which the promise made is meaningless. Is the real reason for this channel-hopping culture actually the revolt against the finitude of human existence?

In the same way, one might ask whether the implausibility of sexual abstinence as a lifestyle choice today is not also a consequence of the futile yearning to taste the whole range of human potentialities within a single life. Could the disgust that sinful human beings feel toward the limits of their created nature also be the reason that we no longer talk of "old people" but "senior citizens"? The older we get, the more we see options being closed off to us: we are forced to let go of certain childhood dreams forever. It is true that old age brings us closer to death, a limit that we rightly rage against, since it is contrary to creation. As a result, aging is an ambiguous process, which in part bears the marks of sin's destructive work. Nevertheless, to dream of eternal youth is to forget our created condition, which is situated in time and part of an ongoing story. Accepting our place as humans also means gratefully accepting the autumn of our life, taking pleasure in the ripe fruits ready for harvest, without lamenting over the paths that life did not allow us to explore and that are now closed to us forever.

Thinking about our finite nature reaches its full depth when we grasp the fact that the limits we encounter as human beings inside creation ultimately point us to the limit that is constitutive of our existence: we are created. Not only are we forbidden from clawing our way up to God's level, but

it is impossible for us to do so. The fact that human beings
are neither omnipresent, nor eternal, nor almighty, serves as
a reminder of our status as created beings. As such, we are
always *secondary* to our Creator; only by this dependence on
the One who made us can we understand ourselves; only in
this way can we live. The meaning of the man's name itself is
a reminder. He is *Adam*, the "earthling," and this place-name
is also an indicator of humankind's status as created beings:
"The heavens are the LORD's heavens, but the earth he has given
to the sons of Adam" (Psalm 115:16; compare Ecclesiastes 5:2).
As we have seen, creaturehood is not a constraint, an enslaving
restriction. On the contrary, it is a blessing, and it defines a
mission. How liberating it is to submit to the Lord of creation,
the Lord of history! Human beings are made for this. Instead
of pursuing unattainable and ultimately destructive fantasies,
by accepting our place we find the framework in which we
can live our existence to the full.

VIII

DISTINGUISHING BETWEEN WOMAN AND MAN

◆

VIII

A T THE SAME TIME THAT Scripture
is strongly emphasizing the wholly
good character of all that God has
made, the Genesis account sounds
a vigorous "It is not good" while the creative action is yet
under way: "The LORD God said, 'It is not good that the man
should be alone. I will make him a helper to be his companion' " (Genesis 2:18). As long as the man is alone, the Creator
refrains from placing his seal of approval on his work. This
fact in itself is worth mentioning: it shows man's inherently

social nature, meaning he cannot flourish as long as he has no partner. Solitude is not a sign of independence, but of need. Even God, who is self-sufficient, does not exist in lonely isolation: as the Triune God, he experiences perfect communion within himself. But man, as a created being, cannot be his own companion.

The creation account insists that the man's partner must also be human: when the animals are brought to Adam so he can name them, he has to admit the search has failed: "For himself, the man found no helper to be his companion" (Genesis 2:20). Although animals may keep us company, support us, and enrich our lives, they cannot be true companions, given how different those created in the image of God are from all others. It is tragic for a cat or a dog to be the last friend that someone has left; this is indeed a profound mark of solitude. However, while it is true that animals cannot be true companions for people, God's remark also implies that the vertical relationship, between humans and their Creator, does not suffice either. The man needs a counterpart who is like him so that he can live out the fullness of his human nature. While union with God is constitutive for human beings, it must be reflected horizontally in relationships with other people. It is tragic to be "Mr. All-alone"[36]: we are dependent on one another. This is why the family, the neighborhood, and other networks that bring people together are so important. It also means we have a responsibility to be a neighbor to others:

being attentive to those who are isolated and lonely, and not deceiving ourselves by thinking that we can get along perfectly well without other people.

While God's statement "it is not good" confirms humanity's social nature, the story gives an additional clarification to which we should pay attention: to remedy the man's solitude, God does not create another man, but a woman. The fact that the first relationship between two humans in the Bible is between a man and a woman highlights the otherness that is necessary in any relationship: when I want the other person to be identical to me, or to be no more than the image that I have of them, a real relationship of love and trust is impossible. The other person can only be my counterpart if they are different from me, while sharing the same human nature.

What is true of all human relationships appears most clearly in the one where woman and man are face-to-face. The Bible's origin accounts make much of the differentiation of the sexes. Human beings are made in two distinct sexes; they are either male or female: "God created man in his own image. ... Male and female he created them" (Genesis 1:27). The Scriptures leave no room for the idea of the androgynous human, which we find in mythology: one person can never recapitulate the whole of human experience and skills; they always need to be complemented, to be helped. The Swiss theologian Karl Barth reminds us that the difference between the sexes is the only one the Bible mentions in reference to the creation of humanity.[37]

◆ ◆ ◆

The Greek myth of the androgynous human

In the first place, there were three sexes among men, not two as now, male and female, but a third sex in addition, being both of them in common ... androgynous both in form and name. ... The form of each human being as a whole was round, with back and sides forming a circle, but it had four arms and an equal number of legs, and two faces exactly alike on a cylindrical neck; there was a single head for both faces, which faced in opposite directions, and four ears and two sets of pudenda, and one can imagine all the rest from this. ... The male originally was the offspring of the Sun, the female of the Earth, and what has a share of both of the Moon, because the Moon also has share of both. ... They were terrible in strength and force, and they had high thoughts and conspired against the gods. ...

Zeus and the other gods took counsel about what they ought to do, and were at a loss, for they didn't see how they could kill them ... because the honors and sacrifices they received from human beings would disappear—nor yet could they allow them to act so outrageously. After thinking very hard indeed, Zeus said, "I believe I've got a device by which men may continue to exist and yet stop their intemperance, namely, by becoming weaker. I'll now cut each of them in two ..." Now when their nature was divided in two, each half in longing rushed to the other half of itself and they threw their arms around each other and intertwined them, desiring to grow together into one, dying of hunger and inactivity too because they were unwilling to do anything apart from one another. ...

But Zeus took pity and provided another device, turning their pudenda to the front—for up till then they had those on the outside ... for this reason: so that if male met female, they might in their embrace beget and their race continue to exist, while at the same time if male met male, there'd at least be satiety from their intercourse and they'd be relieved and go back to work and look after the other concerns of life. So Eros for each other is inborn in people from as long ago as that, and he unites their ancient nature, undertaking to make one from two, and to heal human nature.

THE SPEECH OF ARISTOPHANUS,
FROM PLATO'S *SYMPOSIUM*,
CIRCA 385 BC[38]

◆ ◆ ◆

This fact, which relativizes all other distinctions (such as those of class or ethnicity), emphasizes the structural role of sexual difference, long before Freud and the findings of modern psychology. The Bible thus goes against the blurring of the sexes: being male or female affects the whole person; it is not a minor distinction that is limited to a few physiological differences.

No one can deny that sexual differentiation lies at the heart of countless sorrows. Literature—like life—overflows with stories of broken hearts. Likewise, the place of women, in marriage and in society, has often been characterized by oppression and exploitation. The atmosphere at the beginning of Genesis stands in stark contrast to the weight of painful experience. Here, the man receives the woman as a gift from God and rejoices at the sight of Eve, created "bone of [his] bones and flesh of [his] flesh," who is thus the true answer to his solitude (Genesis 2:23). Their difference is in no way a pretext for subjugation, but an opportunity for meeting and fellowship. The creation accounts are quite explicit: sexual differentiation is created by God; it is therefore good, like all his work. It is true that after creation, sin profoundly disrupted the created order. Nevertheless, the reciprocity between men and women is a God-given gift, one that we must learn to live out in the light of the Bible's teaching.

As to the status of the woman, Genesis vigorously teaches a dual truth that characterizes all that the Bible says on this subject. First, the woman possesses the same nature, the same vocation, and the same dignity as the man. In fact, the first creation account does not mention any difference between the sexes. It is true that it states the fact that humanity exists in masculine and feminine forms. But the text does not reserve any special treatment for the woman: together with the man, she is created in the image and likeness of God. The mission to procreate and have dominion over the earth is given to both; the same food is allotted to them (Genesis 1:26–30). This egalitarian treatment is all the more remarkable given that the first readers lived in a society that emphasized the difference between the sexes far more strongly than ours today. We can conclude from this that the woman is first and foremost *human*; her femininity (and by implication the man's masculinity) is always a secondary distinction within their shared humanity. As a result, neither women nor men should be confined to the roles of "feminine" and "masculine": both are created to live in relationship with their Creator and to fulfill the earthly vocation that humanity has received. The apostle Peter writes that women are "fellow heirs of the grace of [eternal] life" (1 Peter 3:7). In contrast to other religious conceptions (which persist to this day), the Scriptures do not teach any male privilege concerning communion with God or salvation. To quote the *Westminster Shorter Catechism*'s opening question, woman's chief end, like man's, "is to glorify God and enjoy him forever."[39] To this we can add the duty of serving together: the equality between men and women is not only expressed by their common salvation, but also by a blessing and a mission that they must undertake together.

Although Genesis 2 looks more closely at the distinction between the sexes, it does so in the context of a shared humanity. We have already mentioned the joyous delight of the man when he meets the woman and finds her to be like him: "bone of my bones and flesh of my flesh." We also see that the man has no active part in the creation of the woman—he is fast asleep at that point. He then welcomes her as the companion he has been given: the woman is not man's creation; both come from God. One might wonder whether the woman's being made from the man's rib is another symbol of the equality of the two sexes. Many commentators have understood it this way: "God did not make the woman 'out of the man's head to rule over him, nor out of his feet to be trampled upon by him, but out of his side to be equal with him, under his arm to be protected, and near his heart to be beloved.' "[40]

The second creation account goes beyond the truth of man and woman's shared humanity; it teaches the difference between the two. It thus provides the emblematic expression of the Bible's second truth about woman: she is man's counterpart, one who is different from him. More accurately, their relationship is not one of indeterminate symmetry, with man and woman side-by-side, in an egalitarian relationship where the roles are interchangeable. No; in the image of the God of order, their relationship is structured: it reveals a created *order.* The woman is not only different from the man, but, let us dare to use the word, she is *second* to him, not in value or dignity, but in the ordering of creation.

Several clues in the text lead to this proposition. The most remarkable feature concerns the reason why woman is made: she is created because of man. The order in which the two human beings are created and the manner of their creation are closely related to their purpose: the woman is created after the man and from him because she is his helper. Needless to say, there is no reason to deduce from this any inferiority on her part. If anyone is inadequate here, it is the man! The expression translated "helper" is typically used for God when he assists people; it does not suggest a subordinate state. Nevertheless, the account indicates the woman's orientation toward the man. It is true that this orientation is subordinate to the primary truth that man and woman are the image of God. But in the context of an equal dignity and a shared vocation, the roles of the two sexes are not interchangeable.

This understanding of the Genesis account is reinforced by apostolic authority. Paul does not permit a woman to have dominion over a man, citing the fact that Eve was created after Adam (1 Timothy 2:13). Similarly, he finds the confirmation of the statement that "the head of a wife is her husband" in the fact that woman was created "from man" and "for man" (1 Corinthians 11:3, 8–9). The apostle admirably maintains the balance between the two fundamental truths—equality and ordered difference—when he then reminds us that "woman is not without man, nor man without woman, [since both are] in the Lord. For as woman was created from the man, so man is born of woman and everything is from God" (1 Corinthians 11:11–12). The order between man and woman does not harden into a hierarchy because it is not the last word about the sexes. It is based on the work of the transcendent Creator, from whom all things come and who assigns the role of each, in the harmonious totality of a creation that is united by its common origin.

Other elements of the Genesis story support this interpretation. First of all, the dual commandment that God gives to the man, when he tells him from which trees of the garden he may eat, equally applies to the woman. When she breaks it, she is guilty (Genesis 3:2–3). Subsequently, the man gives the woman her name. The close relationship between the words that Adam employs for "man" and "woman" is reflected in English (albeit using a prefix rather than a suffix): "She shall be called *'iššâ* [woman], for from *'îš* [man] she was taken" (Genesis 2:23). While the similarity of the names again emphasizes their common nature, the fact that the man names the woman implies a certain ordering. Finally, the woman expects the man to take the initiative in establishing a new family unit: it is the man who will leave his parents in order to hold fast to his wife (Genesis 2:24).

Asserting that woman is second to man according to the creational order does not go down well today. We should acknowledge that some of the difficulty we feel in this area is for legitimate reasons: too often, the idea of submission has been used, and continues to be used, as a justification for the oppression of women. A Madagascan student told me that some Christians maintain to this day the ancestral custom whereby the wife must serve her husband his meal while she kneels, and only eat what he decides to leave! Such treatment has no justification in the creational order; it is a sign of the disordering of the relationship between the two sexes that results in the man's domineering control over the woman since the fall: "Your desire shall be for your husband, but he shall rule over you" (Genesis 3:16). On the contrary, men are to follow the example of Christ who, out of love, gave his life in sacrifice: "Husbands, love your wives, just as Christ also loved the Church and gave himself for her" (Ephesians 5:25). Far from giving men the right to exploit women, the creational order implies reciprocal duties and provides the context in which men and women can enjoy the harmonious collaboration that their difference makes possible when willingly accepted.

The fact that this order has been abused—and sadly, history provides us with abundant evidence of this—does not prevent the order itself from being good, or negate that men and women have every reason to live it out harmoniously. Seen in this context, the emancipation of women, which has so thoroughly revolutionized the relationship between the sexes, proves to be ambiguous in nature. On the one hand, the aim of women's liberation is equality of both sexes: women are not inferior beings who can only exist under the guardianship of men. In this sense, emancipation fulfills an important aspect of the Bible's teaching about humanity. Some Christians joined this cause very early on; the Salvation Army, to name but one example, granted positions of responsibility to women right from its founding in 1878. But on the other hand, the emancipation is all too often conceived as erasing the differences between men and women. In this scheme, the liberated woman stands as a rival to men and refuses the complementarity of the two sexes in different areas of life, and particularly in the family. The refusal of female particularity leads to a result similar to that of the oppression of the past: ultimately, there is a denial of the woman as *woman*.

The problem is not new: the Greco-Roman society of the first century AD was rife with currents that belittled the roles of wife and mother and encouraged women's presence in public life.[41] The apostle Paul exhorted Christians not to confuse equality in Christ with the removal of all distinctions: although female believers played an active role in worship, prayer, and prophecy, they were not to claim for themselves positions of authority, nor were they to shirk their marital and family responsibilities. It is in this context that Paul points back to the creational order that assigns men and women their respective positions, so that their communion and service might be harmonious (1 Corinthians 11:3–16; 14:33–40; 1 Timothy 2:15).[42]

Since sexual differentiation structures the whole person, the creational order informs the relationships between men and women in the various spheres of human existence. Not only must each couple find an appropriate way to embody this order, but the father and mother each have a specific role to play in educating their children. It will also affect the way that they serve in different ministries at church, as well as the necessary balance between public and family commitments. Although the Bible does not limit women to family responsibilities—the wife of noble character of Proverbs 31 is a businesswoman as much as she is a housewife—the Genesis account suggests differing priorities. The judgment that God pronounces on the first human couple, after their rebellion, distinguishes the areas in which they will be most affected: the woman in the marital relationship and in childbearing, the man in his relationship to the work of shaping his environment (Genesis 3:16–19).[43] We can deduce from this that men and women each make a particular contribution in the outworking of their common vocation to procreate and have dominion over the earth. Their respective roles are not interchangeable.

To understand the full extent of the Bible's teaching on the role of women, it is not enough to think about the creational order only as it concerns human relationships. In seeking to understand how woman can be both equal and second to man, we should remember that the Trinity contains within it the archetype of all ordered relationships between equals. The apostle Paul explicitly compares the relationship between the Father and the Son with that between man and woman: "The husband is the head of the wife; God is the head of Christ" (1 Corinthians 11:3). The Son being second to the Father in the Trinity provides us with the supreme example of an ordered relationship that does not contain the least trace of inferiority. Thinking about the order of man and woman in light of the Trinity makes absolutely clear that this order has nothing to do with any sort of humiliation of the woman; it is only when this order is distorted that there is exploitation and abasement. The creational order, on the contrary, is the context in which love can flourish, so that man and woman together are able to embrace their shared vocation to worship and serve the Lord, each representing a facet of the divine life.

The mystery of the Trinity points us to the mystery of creation: just as, from all eternity, God has his own image within himself, so he creates, freely and inside time, the world that is distinct from him. Insofar as God is not the solitary God of unitary monotheism, but of communion as well as unity, he can bring into existence created beings that are truly distinct from him and produce a universe composed of a plurality of beings. The doctrine of creation is thus strongly linked to the doctrine of the Trinity. As early as the Genesis account, we see indications of the Trinity at work in the act of creation: while the divine Word participates as the means of creation, "the

Spirit of God hovered over the face of the waters" (Genesis 1:2). Even if we should resist the temptation to see in these verses a comprehensive revelation of the Trinity, the plural of divine deliberation—"let us make man" (Genesis 1:26)—counts as an additional clue to suggest, from the very first page of the Bible, that God is not solitary.

Since the harmonious order of the three divine persons is reflected in the relationship between man and woman, we should expect the latter to express something of the mystery of creation. It is not at all surprising, therefore, that in the Bible sexual differentiation is symbolic of the distinction between the Creator and created beings. The verse from 1 Corinthians we have already considered contains a third parallel proposition: "Christ is the head of every man" (11:3). The structure of the verse suggests a comparison between three similar pairs of relations: between the Father and the Son, between the Creator and the world (represented by human beings), and between man and woman. The Old Testament uses sexual differentiation symbolically and often describes the covenant God makes with his people in terms of marriage. The apostle Paul echoes this usage when he applies the image to the relationship between Christ and his church, which is a new humanity, representing creation: " 'For this reason a man will leave his father and mother and hold fast to his wife, and the two will become one flesh.' This mystery is great; I apply it to Christ and the Church" (Ephesians 5:31–32).[44]

To understand the symbolic value of sexual differentiation, we can imagine a painting in which the painter represents himself painting the picture we are looking at. In a similar way, God has placed inside creation an image of the relationship that he maintains with the world: as the woman is different from the man, so created human beings find themselves before God. This symbolic interpretation of sexual distinction guides Paul's exposition in Romans 1, where he establishes a close link between idolatry and homosexuality. After castigating the lie of idolatry that worships and serves "the creature instead of the Creator," he immediately turns to the question of sexual disordering: "For this reason God gave them over to dishonorable passions: their wives exchanged natural relations for unnatural ones; in the same way, the men, leaving natural relations with women, were inflamed with desire for one another" (Romans 1:25–27). Admittedly, Paul goes on to mention other sins that result from the refusal to worship the true God, but why does he place such emphasis on homosexuality? The answer is found in the symbolic value of sexual differentiation: what homosexuality is in the interpersonal domain, idolatry is in the religious domain. Both amount to a denial of a fundamental otherness; on the one hand, between man and woman, on the other, between God and created things. Since sexual differentiation is the symbol of the distinction between the Creator and the world, idolatry that confuses the two has as a logical consequence the refusal to recognize the inalienable distinction between the sexes. Rejecting the distinctions within creation goes hand in hand with rebelling against the Creator, since the creational order clearly bears the mark of the One who established it.

Discovering the symbolic value of the relationship between the sexes emphasizes once more that there is nothing demeaning for women in the creational order, provided that this order is lived out according to God's purpose and does not become a pretext for men to seize power. On the contrary, it is the framework within which men and women can live out, in complementarity, their shared vocation to worship and serve the Creator. In this respect, each sex has the responsibility of expressing a particular aspect of the shared dignity of being the image of God: "Well did the Creator weigh the respective advantages of the male and the female. The scales are less unequal than is supposed. Each one of us, man and woman, finds it easier to live one dimension of the human portion, being as the image of God; one represents him, one corresponds to him."[45] Since nothing in creation is able, on its own, to express all the fullness of what it means to be created, man and woman must complement each other in order to fully signify what it is to be human: we are called to represent God *and* must live in relationship with him. Refusing the order of man and woman makes it impossible for humanity to fully play its part on the world's stage: this role can only be undertaken together, with both making their own specific contribution, in line with the Creator's plan.

IX

EMBRACING A
FULLY HUMAN
SEXUALITY

◆

IX

SEXUAL DIFFERENTIATION AFFECTS OUR PER-
SONALITIES so deeply that no aspect of human
existence eludes its imprint. Without resorting
to clichés, a woman does not engage with the
outside world, let alone another person, in the same way as
a man does. In any interaction, one's sex has an influence on
the relations that are established. This general fact takes con-
crete form in a particular setting: the act of love that unites
a man and a woman. No other relationship expresses more
deeply the face-to-face partnership between the two sexes,

from creation onwards. It is fitting therefore that the second creation account concludes its teaching on sexual differentiation with what we might call the "marriage charter": "A man shall leave his father and mother, he will hold fast to his wife, and the two shall become one flesh" (Genesis 2:24).

The text indicates three stages in the consummation of love: "leaving," "cleaving," and "becoming one flesh." Each stage is important in its own way; none of them should be left out if we want love to be able to flourish. Let us start with the first one: the text shows that the consummation of love is preceded by a public act in which the man *leaves* the parental home to start a new social unit with his wife. Throughout history, societies have developed different customs for the marriage ceremony; despite their diverse forms, all declare that the love between a man and a woman is not a private affair but constitutes a public commitment. Only in this way can love endure and be protected by the community. Although marriage is a commitment between two people, it must also be respected by everyone else: on the one hand, parents must keep the necessary distance for the young couple to flourish, and on the other hand, no hopeful admirers should interfere with the couple's union.

The second stage is about *cleaving*. It concerns the personal dimension of commitment, experienced by the couple themselves: marriage includes both public act and private union. The verb in question has a strong meaning and can

Jesus is questioned about divorce

Pharisees came to test Jesus, saying, "Is it lawful to divorce one's wife for any reason?" He answered, "Have you not read that the Creator, from the beginning, made them male and female and said, 'For this reason a man shall leave his father and mother and hold fast to his wife, and the two shall become one flesh.' So they are no longer two, but one flesh. Therefore, what God has joined together, let not man separate." They said to him, "Why then did Moses command to issue a certificate of divorce in case of repudiation?" He said to them, "It is because of your hardness of heart that Moses allowed you to divorce your wives. But in the beginning, it was not so. I tell you, whoever divorces his wife—except for sexual misconduct—and marries another, commits adultery."

MATTHEW 19:3–9

mean "to stick"; it emphasizes the intensity of the bond that is made. This raises the question of the circumstances under which one can "unstick" what has been joined together in this way. The Pharisees put this very question to Jesus, who quotes the verse from Genesis in his answer as a decisive argument against divorce. He immediately adds the following remark: "So they [the husband and wife] are no longer two, but one flesh. Therefore, what God has joined together, let not man separate" (Matthew 19:5–6). Although marriage is a human act, Jesus indicates that it is God himself who established the institution. Thus the union entered into by human beings takes on a sacred status. Admittedly, marriage is not a sacrament in the usual sense of the word: established at creation, it is part of the arrangements that society must manage. It is not exclusive to the Church; even marriages between unbelievers are fully valid. But since marriage in its civic nature is willed by God, Jesus can say that it is *God* who unites husband and wife in the marital bond. It follows that any breaking of this sacred bond goes against the Creator's plan. Of course, Jesus is realistic enough to know that divorce is sometimes inevitable. In this sense, marriage is not an unbreakable bond—something that is unfortunately confirmed by experience. Adultery, in particular, can sever it and thereby release the other partner from the vows made. But although divorce cannot always be avoided, it is "because of your hardness of heart"; "in the beginning, it was not so" (Matthew 19:8). Every divorce demonstrates the destructive work of sin; it is not an expression of freedom from the commitment made, but a breaking, a rupture, at odds with the creational order. As a result, it is a deeply painful experience. What has been, so to speak, glued together so strongly cannot be unglued without causing harm.

The third stage indicates the place where the marriage is consummated: its deepest expression is manifested by bodily union, sexual relations. Interestingly, the text makes no mention of procreation. Children are a gift from the Lord; they are both a blessing and a mission. By accepting the gift of new life, the married couple participate in the fulfillment of humanity's creational vocation: "Be fruitful ... and fill the earth" (Genesis 1:28). Nevertheless, the second creation account, which makes so much of sexual differentiation, does not say a single word about procreation. We can conclude from this that childbearing is neither the main reason for marriage, nor what makes one valid: a childless marriage is a genuine marriage nonetheless. Infertility is never justification for divorce.

In the biblical worldview, sexuality is lived out in the partnership between a man and a woman. This is not a nostalgic quest for some kind of long-lost original unity, as the Platonic myth of the androgynous human being imagines.[46] Ever since creation, human beings have been either male or female. Therefore, neither men nor women are so-called human halves, each waiting to find their true identity by merging with someone of the opposite sex. We misunderstand the term "one flesh" if we take it as an invitation to a fusional kind of love. Marriage is a *covenant*: it is based on the meeting of two people who acknowledge their complementarity without denying their individuality. The sexual relations that are part of marriage do not only respect the specificities of each partner, they presuppose them. Marriage is built on the difference *par excellence* between human beings: sexual differentiation.

The "marriage charter" situates sexual practice within the context of the marital bond. This fact is a divine arrangement with several implications. First, it assumes an unconditional "yes" to sexuality. Contrary to all ascetic approaches, the Scriptures see sexuality as a gift from the Lord. Granted, the fall has left a deep mark on this area of human nature—as it has on all the others. But the ways we see sex being misused (and in which we are implicated, to a greater or lesser extent) must never lead us to forget that sexuality itself comes from the Creator's hand. The intensity of the suffering caused can even be considered proportional to the value of the gift: the reason that deviating from God's plan for sex is so damaging is because sexual differentiation is such an important part of who we are as people.

Second, the context God defines for sexual relations implies a radical restriction. For those who are married, the choice of a partner is narrowed to a single option: the spouse, necessarily of the opposite sex. Extramarital affairs or polygamy have no place in the Creator's plan. It is true that for a time, God tolerated the custom of polygamy. When, in a society, the position of single women is extremely precarious, polygamous marriage might be preferable to no protection at all. This is why too sudden a break from this custom, if it is deeply rooted in the fabric of society, could do more harm than good. However, the stories of polygamous families that are told in the following chapters of Genesis leave us in no doubt: straying from God's initial plan in creation leads to great emotional pain. The sending away of Hagar (whom Sarah herself had chosen for her husband Abraham as a second wife), and the rivalry between Jacob's wives, both provide poignant proof that polygamy is not a setting in which love can flourish (Genesis 16:29–30). The apostle Paul's command is in line with the Creator's intention: "Let every man have his own wife, and every woman her own husband" (1 Corinthians 7:2).

For those who are unmarried, the Genesis passage—as confirmed by the rest of the Bible—implies sexual abstinence. This requirement obviously goes against the grain of our society, where permissiveness is the norm. However, Christians know whom they are to obey, convinced that God's law is *good*. This trust is sufficient for them to live their lives in accordance with the Creator's instructions. But is it possible to go further and understand why God ordained this restriction? Three considerations can help us here.

First, the human person is a unified whole: one cannot separate the physical act from either the psychological experience or the spiritual dimension of the individual. Therefore, sexuality is not an animalistic desire that can be satisfied while disregarding the other dimensions of the human person. It must be exercised in a *humane* way, with respect for both oneself and one's partner. Marital faithfulness alone provides the setting in which sexuality can take on this characteristic, sustaining and nourishing the couple's relationship in the different aspects of married life. This is why the apostle Paul denounces the way in which the Christians in Corinth took prostitution so lightly, likely influenced by (pre-)Gnostic ideas,[47] which dissociated spirituality from the body and denigrated the material aspect of the human condition. Paul uses a verse from Genesis as a decisive argument against using sexuality in such a compartmentalized manner: "Do you not know that he who is joined to a prostitute becomes one body with her? For it is written, 'The two shall become one flesh.' But he who is joined to the Lord is one spirit with him. Flee from sexual immorality' " (1 Corinthians 6:16–18). Since sexual differentiation structures our whole being, bodily union cannot be restricted to the physical dimension: it is a commitment of all that we are. Sexual activity cannot be separated from the other dimensions of the person. Therefore, physical union must presuppose and undergird the joining of lives in the context of marriage.

A second consideration is also related to the structural role of sexuality: the constitutive depth of sexual differentiation means that sexual desire is of crucial importance and significant force. It is therefore necessary to set limits on it so that it does not take over the whole of existence and in doing so prevent the development of the rest of human potential. Both individuals and society as a whole need boundaries to ensure sexual practice has its proper place. The precision of the setting to which it is limited thus indicates the essential role that sexual differentiation plays in human nature.

The third consideration prevents us from overplaying the importance of sex and thus serves as a counterbalance to the two previous remarks. In order to do justice to the coherence of the Bible's teaching, we must not only acknowledge the structural importance of sexual differentiation but also recognize that it plays out in the context of a common humanity: man and woman are first of all *human beings*; masculinity and femininity are but secondary determinations. Therefore, the exercise of one's sexuality is not essential for the fulfillment of the human vocation; someone who refrains from sexual relations is not any less human. The same is true of sexual determination: a person's masculinity, or femininity, is not diminished by a life of sexual abstinence. It is important to repeat this truth in an age where celibacy is often looked upon with disdain. In many traditional societies, marriage is the gateway to the adult world; the idea that it is possible to live an independent, fulfilled life as a single person is inconceivable. While it is true that celibacy is less of a problem in modern Western society, it comes at the price of impurity: those who voluntarily embrace chastity are met with incomprehension. It is imperative that we recover the balance of the Bible's teaching on sex: while the Scriptures in no way promote an ascetic lifestyle, they also refute those who see sex as the ultimate goal of life, something without which we cannot fulfill our human nature. Let us not forget: Jesus Christ carried out his earthly ministry while remaining celibate—Jesus, the man *par excellence*! Single Christians can be grateful that their lifestyle is the same as their Master's. In respecting the restriction that God has imposed, they communicate in a very tangible way that even the most passionate romantic love cannot fully satisfy humanity's deepest aspirations. Human beings are first and foremost created for God; all other determinations are secondary in the light of this ultimate truth. That is why it is worth obeying one's Creator rather than giving in to the desire for human companionship, even though the latter is so deeply wired into our nature. Unmarried Christians can accept, without being ashamed of it, the feeling that they lack something,[48] without making the mistake of trying to satisfy this need outside of God's good plan. In this way, their choice of sexual abstinence becomes a compelling testament to the fact that our relationship with the Creator has priority over all others.

X

ENTERING INTO GOD'S REST

◆

X

THE SECOND CREATION ACCOUNT CONCLUDES with the marital harmony of the first couple: "The man and his wife were both naked, and they felt no shame" (Genesis 2:25). In parallel to this harmony, the first account culminates in God's Sabbath: "Thus were completed the heavens and the earth, with all they contain. God finished, on the seventh day, his work that he had done, and he rested, on the seventh day, from all his work that he had done. He blessed the seventh day and made it holy, for on that day, he rested from all the work that he had done by way of creation" (Genesis 2:1–3). Both stories end, in their own way, on an image of perfect peace and fulfillment.

How should we understand the fact that God rested? The text bears no mention of any tiredness that needed alleviating by the seventh day. The work of creation is carried out without any resistance whatsoever; God's mere word is followed by results that correspond perfectly to his expressed will. The reason the author uses the daring anthropomorphism of rest, of the cessation of activity, is to underline the perfection of the work: God does not need to be continually repairing creation, like an incompetent inventor who has to constantly fix a badly designed machine. It is true that sin enters at a later point and disrupts the world's harmonious equilibrium. But sin does not exploit any inherent flaw in creation; it is a *historical* act of free created beings. The structures of reality do not provide any excuse for this. God is in no way responsible for this inexplicable rebellion. Human beings, placed in a perfect environment—"very good," according to the narrative (Genesis 1:31)—cannot point to any lack, any deficiency, to justify their rebellion against the Creator.

God's rest from his work is not absolute: when Jesus is accused of healing on the Sabbath and therefore breaking the law of Moses, he justifies his actions by explaining that he is merely imitating the work of his heavenly Father: "My Father is working until now, and I also am working. ... Amen, amen,

I say to you, the Son can do nothing of his own accord, but only what he sees the Father doing; for whatever the Father does, the Son also does likewise" (John 5:17, 19). Jesus's reasoning is based on the assumption that God is active on the Sabbath. If we detect here an allusion to Genesis, we may conclude that this seventh day is equivalent to all of history—it lasts "until now," Jesus implies. In fact, the attentive reader cannot help but notice that it does not end, as the other days do, with the refrain: "And there was evening, and there was morning, the nth day." There is no eighth day following God's Sabbath.

The survival of the world depends on its Creator never ceasing to be actively present in it. The psalmist sings of God's indispensable providence in the strongest of terms (Psalm 104:27–30):

All look to you,
   to give them their food in due season.
You give it to them, they gather it up;
   you open your hand, they are filled with good things.
You hide your face, they are terrified;
   you take away their breath,
   they expire and return to dust.
You send your breath, they are created;
   you renew the face of the earth.

Unlike the deists' idea of the Great Watchmaker, God did not set the world going at creation and then leave it to run its predetermined course. In fact, all creatures are dependent on their Creator to such an extent that they cannot exist, even for a moment, without the Lord's sustaining action.

However, providence does not mean continual creation. God's rest on the seventh day marks a difference between the two regimes: in his providence, God sustains the world with its created structures, which are already established and stable. The world is not a mirage, a dreamlike image that God produces moment by moment, without any connection to what came before. Although created beings continually depend on God, they still possess real existence. It follows that God's providence is mediated by a network of reliable laws of nature, which allow human beings to direct their action in the world. Providence is therefore characterized by two elements that distinguish it from creation. First, while creation brings forth qualitative novelties, providence maintains the different realms of the created order: earth and sky; dry land and sea; plant, animal, and human life. Second, while creation establishes creational laws, providence is their continuation. This distinction is not absolute, however, since creation undoubtedly also involved natural means—Genesis mentions, for example, that the *earth* produced vegetation (Genesis 1:11). God's Sabbath, however, prevents us from considering the two systems as identical.

The divine Sabbath is not simply a day of rest: God blesses it and declares it holy. The scope of the blessing in which God had placed animals and humans is enlarged and takes on a cosmic dimension: God declares his approval of all that he has made and, so to speak, wishes it well. The whole history that unfolds from creation onward is thus characterized by blessing. The created beings can enter into it with confidence, since the wish of the Creator himself is that things go well. The seventh day that is declared *holy* emphasizes once more that this blessedness cannot be achieved outside of fellowship with God. Holiness means belonging to the Lord, and this is expressed in worship. God's blessing therefore creates a "space" of sanctified existence, and the only coherent response from human beings is worship. They cannot experience true fulfillment unless they live in joyful celebration of their dependence on God.

The Creator's desire that his creation be blessed should not be seen as merely wishful thinking, since as Lord of heaven and earth, he has the power to accomplish his plans. While it is true that what follows shows the humanity's rebellion, seeking an illusory independence rather than life-giving dependence on the Creator, sin cannot thwart God's original plan. Even though we must now take the circuitous route via the cross of Christ, "there remains a Sabbath rest for the people of God," as the Epistle to the Hebrews puts it (4:9). The Creator remains in control of history and ensures that his plan for blessing will succeed. He sets out on the path of redemption so that humanity might reconnect with the divine blessing, which they rebelled against to their own misfortune.

The Genesis account has human beings appearing on the day before the Sabbath. What should we conclude from this detail of the story? The creation of humans on the sixth day—rather than the seventh—contains, first of all, a word of humility: humanity is not the goal of creation toward which all of nature points. Our coming into existence is part of a larger whole, one whose ultimate horizon is transcendent: "The heavens declare the glory of God"—not the glory of humanity (Psalm 19:1). The universe celebrates its Creator, and human beings are called to join this cosmic concert, as worshipers and not the ones being worshiped! Consequently, we find that we are primarily receivers of our human condition rather than agents of it. As created beings, humans receive everything that constitutes the basis of our existence—our life; our physical, emotional, and intellectual potential; our name and family—before ever doing anything that might affect our own situation. In the creation account, the Sabbath precedes human response to their calling: though humanity is called to be fruitful, to fill the earth and subdue it, it can only do so on the basis of the gifts it has received and in the setting established by the Creator.

What might at first appear to be a devaluing of human effort turns out to be profoundly liberating. This call to humility reveals as superfluous any effort we might expend trying to establish our existence ourselves, to prove our right to exist. There is nothing to prove—to others, nor to ourselves. Our value does not stem from what we achieve, but from our dignity as beings created as God's image. The New Testament confirms this understanding of the Sabbath: Hebrews 4 draws a parallel between Sabbath rest and justification by faith and not works. God has performed a complete, perfect work—first in creation, then in salvation by the cross of Christ. Our efforts, therefore, are never an attempt to improve on what God has done as if it were in some way inadequate. Understood this way, our work is never more than a voluntary response to the abundance of riches we have received; it is possible only because God provides us with the necessary strength and abilities. Seen from this perspective, the failure of modern societies to acknowledge the dignity of those labeled economically unproductive takes on a different appearance. Could it be that the loss of the transcendent dimension has left us unable to recognize the disabled, the sick, and the elderly as fully human persons, with their potentialities and rich inner lives? Acknowledging that we are created beings frees us from the obligation of justifying our own existence; the love we have freely received from the Creator is all the justification we need.

In the origin account, God's Sabbath comes soon after his declaration of creation's perfect goodness. God can rest from his work because he sees that it is "very good" (Genesis 1:31). We can detect in the Creator's appreciation of the world his satisfaction with the finished work. Since the Sabbath rest is the first work that humans are called to participate in, they share in the Creator's joy. In the same way that God delights in the perfection of his work, humans can in turn rejoice in the full goodness of creation. At a time when most people's lifestyle is urban rather than rural, it is worth saying that gazing at beautiful landscapes is not the only way of experiencing awe and wonder at the creation, even though these are part of its splendor. Even in a environment largely constructed by humans, it is possible for us to share in the joy the Creator takes in his work. First, isn't it true that towns and cities have the advantage of a concentration of the creation's masterpiece, human beings? Not for nothing does Revelation present the future of humanity not in a garden, but in a city: the new Jerusalem (Revelation 21:2). The city alone can provide the redeemed multitude with a suitable setting for fellowship with each other and with God. Second, human technical and artistic achievements are an extension of creation, as long as they are not motivated by revolt against the created order, because they exercise the creative faculties that God has given us, bringing out the potentialities that the act of creation sketched in outline. Moreover, progress in these fields inevitably relies on the structures of the created order to succeed: one can only command nature by obeying its laws, as the English philosopher Francis Bacon (1561–1626) observed. Therefore, a sophisticated piece of technology or an example of beautiful architecture also provide opportunities to celebrate God's good creation.

The Sinai covenant takes God's Sabbath as the basis for observing a weekly day of rest, for the Israelites and all those living in their sphere of influence. This commandment is the fourth of the ten "words" that function as the covenant constitution: "Remember the Sabbath day, to keep it holy. For six days, you shall labor and do all your work. But the seventh day is a Sabbath to the LORD your God. You shall not do any work, neither you, nor your son, nor your daughter, nor your male servant, nor your female servant, nor your cattle, nor the foreigner that dwells with you. For in six days the LORD made heaven and earth, the sea and all that is in them, then he rested on the seventh day. Therefore the LORD blessed the seventh day and made it holy" (Exodus 20:8–11). This commandment was so important that breaking it was an offense that carried the death penalty (Exodus 35:2).

This raises the important question of the scope of the fourth commandment's validity: Should it be understood as a permanent prescription that applies to all times and places? The argument employed by the passage, which grounds the rule in the structure of God's work of creation, has led many theologians to answer in the affirmative. However, the New Testament writings offer little support for this view. For the apostle Paul, Sabbath observance (like that of other feast days) is a matter where differing practices may legitimately coexist within the church: "One person esteems one day as more important than another, while another esteems them all alike. Each one should be fully convinced in his own mind" (Romans 14:5). Either practice can demonstrate an attitude that glorifies the Lord. It is therefore not appropriate to expect all Christians to have the same approach in this matter.

Taking such liberties with the fourth commandment may seem surprising when we remember how severely any deviation from it was punished. However, the contrasting position that Paul takes becomes clearer when we understand the role the Sabbath plays in the economy of salvation: along with other commandments, like the dietary rules and the sacrificial system, it is one of the means that God used to prepare his people for the definitive revelation in Christ. These were "a shadow of things to come, but the reality is Christ" (Colossians 2:17). In particular, the Sabbath was a reminder to the Israelites that they had received everything: their existence as human beings in this world created by God, and their special status as a people dedicated to the service and worship of the Lord (Exodus 31:12–17). He thus prepared them for the concept of freely given salvation. Now that redemption has been accomplished by the cross of Christ, the systems that prefigured it can disappear. New covenant believers live each day with the joy of salvation by grace; God's blessing encompasses their whole existence, so that for them, every day becomes a Sabbath on which they can rest in God's goodness and rejoice in his works.

◆ ◆ ◆

John Calvin on the meaning of the Sabbath

First, under the repose of the seventh day the heavenly
Lawgiver meant to represent to the people of Israel spiritual rest, in which believers ought to lay aside their own
works to allow God to work in them.

Secondly, he meant that there was to be a stated day
for them to assemble to hear the law and perform the
rites, or at least to devote it particularly to meditation
upon his works, and thus through this remembrance to
be trained in piety.

Thirdly, he resolved to give a day of rest to servants
and those who are under the authority of others, in order
that they should have some respite from toil.

JOHN CALVIN,
INSTITUTES OF THE CHRISTIAN RELIGION[49]

◆ ◆ ◆

Let us not, however, be too quick to dismiss the idea of a weekly rest day: the disappearance of the Sabbath as a pointer to salvation in Christ should not cause us to neglect the beneficial cycle of work and rest. Human beings need to organize their lives and find practical ways to enjoy the freedom that comes from not having to prove our worth by our work. This need is heightened by our social nature: when a society agrees on a common day of rest, its quality increases. Those who have to work on Sundays know that a day off during the week does not really make up for it, either in physical rest or having a social life. This is why the second version of the Ten Commandments, in the book of Deuteronomy, bases the Sabbath law on a social reason: the Israelites needed to remember how harsh the slavery they had endured in Egypt was, so that they would be motivated to observe the common day of rest—"So your male servant and your female servant will be able to rest as you do" (Deuteronomy 5:14).

The first Christians were well aware of the importance of a weekly rhythm in structuring human activity: we see indications in the New Testament that, very early on, the church made a habit of meeting on Sundays for worship (Acts 20:7; 1 Corinthians 16:2; Revelation 1:10). It is true that this was not yet a day of *rest*: the number of Christians was too small to have this kind of influence on society. In any case, from the Bible's perspective, rest is not just about recharging our physical and mental batteries but means setting aside time to maintain interpersonal relationships and enjoy communion with God. Making Sunday a special day of celebration thus confirms the validity of commonly accepted structures for the rhythm of human life.

Observing a weekly day of rest can thereby be seen in a new light: the question is not whether we are allowed to work on that day or not. On the contrary, it is up to us to experience it as an invitation to enjoy creation (and salvation): since our human vocation is not just about work, the rhythm of our lives is set by this balance between work and celebration. In this way, a day of rest is not a constraint imposed on us that we must obey legalistically. It provides us—individually and as a society—with space that allows us to rest from our labors, to appreciate the goodness of creation, and to lift our eyes to our Creator. It is most definitely not an invitation to be lazy! This day indeed reminds us that our activity extends the work of creation. Our work finds its true place inside the work that God has already done for us. How could we fulfill such a noble calling by giving anything less than our best? But we will also be able to rest and give the necessary time to those we live with and to the Creator himself. Our labors are only ever *pen*ultimate: the world's future depends on hands that are stronger than ours. Just as God formed the heavens and the earth in the beginning, so it is he who will bring his work to completion at the end of time, when he will make a new heaven and a new earth.

EPILOGUE

*L*ET US LOOK BACK ON the road we've traveled: thinking about creation from first two chapters of the Bible has led us to examine some of the most diverse aspects of the human condition. From religion to work, from procreation to diet, from marriage to science—no aspect of what humanity is or does is unaffected by the worldview found in Scripture. Despite the number of subjects we have considered, this study can hardly claim to be exhaustive: many other worthy themes have been left untouched. For example, Genesis 2 describes the

man and the woman as naked in their state of original innocence. There is much we could learn from this about the role
of clothing, which, we may recall, was only introduced after
the fall (Genesis 2:25; 3:21)! However, it is time to draw this
study of the origin accounts to a provisional conclusion and
leave for another day the joy of unearthing yet more hidden
treasures from these ancient texts.

One key point that we can take away is that God cares
about our human condition in its entirety. He is, and wants to
be ever-increasingly, the God of our everyday lives. In contrast
to the modern tendency of confining God to a religious com-
partment that has no influence on the rest of our existence, the
Scriptures show us that God will not let himself be relegated to
a corner of our lives, whether as individuals or as a society: as
Creator, he is sovereign over every part of life. Acknowledging
this does not lead to fundamentalist fanaticism, since the doctrine of creation is what prevents the believer from only being
concerned with a narrowly defined, so-called religious dimension. On the contrary, believers will be able to discern God's
work in all diverse aspects of human existence, giving the latter
the attention and care they deserve. In their devotion to God,
Christians will remember that their job is not to establish his
kingdom on earth. They will therefore, patiently and peace-
fully, make whatever contribution they can, knowing that one
day, God himself will bring to completion that which is not
yet perfect. In their endeavors, believers will be able to apply

all that they learn through reflecting on creation, because creation provides the guidance that their actions need.

The prophet Zechariah concludes his visions with the surprising promise that one day, all the pots and pans, even the most ordinary ones, will be used to worship the Lord, and so have the same status as the holy vessels in the temple (Zechariah 14:20–21). When God's work of redeeming the world is completed, there will no longer be any distinction between sacred and profane. The world will possess once again the harmony it had at first, and its totality will participate in worship of the Creator. In the meantime, God calls us to let every part of our lives be shaped by faith: "Whether you eat or drink, or whatever you do, do it all for the glory of God" (1 Corinthians 10:31). This is the doctrine of creation's most far-reaching and weighty consequence: every part of our lives, even the most mundane, is an opportunity to worship the One by whom and for whom we were made.

STUDY QUESTIONS

The following questions can help in thinking further about the issues raised by this book. These are intended for both personal study and group discussion.

Chapter I: Recognizing God as the Absolute Origin

1. What alternative understandings of the world's origins does the doctrine of creation rule out?

2. How does Genesis 1 challenge all forms of idolatry?

3. What difference does believing that God is Creator make in our prayer life?

Chapter II: Accepting Existence as a Gift

1. How is the worldview we see in *Nausea* different from Christians' approach to reality?

2. In what practical ways can we express our gratitude, if we know we have received everything?

Chapter III: Inhabiting an Existing Order

1. How does Genesis 1 express the natural order established by the act of creation?

2. How do we distinguish between legitimate and illegitimate uses of technology?

3. In what ways does the doctrine of creation shed light on the environmental issues of our day?

4. How does creation help us to understand human knowledge?

Chapter IV: Understanding Human Dignity

1. How do the creation accounts show humanity's solidarity with the rest of creation? What are the practical implications of this?

2. What expressions and images do the creation accounts employ to teach us what makes human beings special? What consequences might there be for the way we live and behave?

Chapter V: Entering into God's Blessing

1. How does understanding that children are a gift from the Lord (Psalm 127:3) change the way we view them?

2. Can all professions or trades be a suitable response to humanity's creational vocation to work?

3. How does the Bible's teaching about food help us to tackle eating disorders, both for the individual, and as a societal issue?

Chapter VI: Obeying God's Commandment

1. How can we put into practice the command to enjoy the goodness of creation? What are the dangers to avoid as we do so?

2. How can we live out the fear of the Lord today? What are some pitfalls to avoid?

3. Which of God's commandments do you find particularly demanding to keep?

Chapter VII: Accepting Your Limits

1. How can we discern which limitations come from creation versus those that are the result of sin?

2. What human limitation do you have most difficulty accepting? How is the doctrine of creation helpful in regard to this?

3. How can we practically show that we have accepted being in second place in relation to God?

Chapter VIII: Distinguishing between Woman and Man

1. How does the beginning of Genesis communicate that men and women are equal? What are the practical consequences of this teaching?

2. How does the beginning of Genesis express the differences between men and women?

3. Is it important to acknowledge that woman is second to man, and not just different to him?

4. How can we express the creational order between men and women in the different aspects of human life? What are the potential dangers?

Chapter IX: Embracing a Fully Human Sexuality

1. What Bible passages allow us to affirm that sexual pleasure is intended by God? Why do many Christians struggle to accept this part of the Bible's teaching?

2. Why, in the Bible, is sex reserved for marriage? Do you find this rule restrictive? Liberating? Demanding? Beneficial?

3. What is the role of singleness in the Bible?

Chapter X: Entering into God's Rest

1. What is a particular moment when you experienced the goodness of creation?

2. What are warning indicators that our work and rest are out of balance?

3. How can we live out the apostle Paul's appeal: "Whether you eat or drink, or whatever you do, do it all for the glory of God" (1 Corinthians 10:31)?

BIBLIOGRAPHY

Ansaldi, Jean. " 'Célibat pour Christ' et sexualité." *Études Théologiques et Religieuses* 67 (1992): 403–15.

Balthasar, Hans Urs von. *The Truth of the World. Vol. 1 of Theo-Logic: Theological Logical Theory.* Translated by Adrian J. Walker. San Francisco: Ignatius Press, 2000.

Barth, Karl. *Church Dogmatics* III.1. Translated by J. W. Edwards, O. Bussey, and H. Knight. Edinburgh: T&T Clark, 1958.

Blocher, Henri. *In the Beginning: The Opening Chapters of Genesis.* Translated by David G. Preston. Downers Grove, IL: InterVarsity, 1984.

———. "Women, Ministry and the Gospel. Hints for a New Paradigm ?" Pages 239–49 in *Women, Ministry and the Gospel. Exploring New Paradigms*. Edited by M. Husbands and T. Larsen. Downers Grove, IVP Academic, 2007.

Boyd, James Robert. *The Westminster Shorter Catechism, with Analysis, Scriptural Proofs, Explanatory and Practical Inferences, and Illustrative Anecdotes*. Philadelphia: Presbyterian Publication Committee, 1854.

Calvin, John. *Institutes of the Christian Religion*. Edited by John T. McNeill. Translated by Ford Lewis Battles. The Library of Christian Classics. 2 vols. Louisville, KY: Westminster John Knox, 2011.

Clavier, Paul. *Dieu sans barbe: vingt et une conversations instructives et amusantes sur la question très disputée de l'existence de Dieu*. Paris: Table Ronde, 2002.

Dalley, Stephanie. *Myths from Mesopotamia: Gilgamesh, The Flood, and Others*. Oxford: Oxford University Press, 1989.

Goldman Jean-Jacques. *Entre gris clair et gris foncé*. Epic, 1987.

———. *Fredericks Goldman Jones*. JRG, 1990.

Eichrodt, Walter. *Theology of the Old Testament*. Translated by J. A. Baker. Old Testament Library. 2 vols. Philadelphia: Westminster John Knox, 1967.

Einstein, Albert. "Physik und Realität." *Franklin Institute Journal* 221 (1936): 313–47. Translated into English, 349–82.

Gisel, Pierre. *La création: essai sur la liberté et la nécessité, l'histoire et la loi, l'homme, le mal et Dieu*. 2nd ed. Geneva: Labor et Fides, 1987.

Hamilton, Victor P. *The Book of Genesis: Chapters 1–17*. New International Commentary of the Old Testament. Grand Rapids: Eerdmans, 1990.

Jaeger, Lydia. *Pour une philosophie chrétienne des sciences*. Nogent-sur-Marne: Institut Biblique de Nogent, 2000.

———. "Se savoir créature." *Théologie évangélique* 4 (2005): 45–58.

Kant, Emmanuel. *Critique of Pure Reason: In Commemoration of the Centenary of Its First Publication*. Translated by Friedrich Max Müller. 2nd ed. New York: Macmillan, 1907.

Kidner, Derek. *Genesis: An Introduction and Commentary*. Tyndale Old Testament Commentaries. London: Tyndale Press, 1967.

Kitchen, Kenneth. *On the Reliability of the Old Testament*. Grand Rapids: Eerdmans, 2003.

Lambert, W. G. *Babylonian Creation Myths*. Mesopotamian Civilizations 16. Winona Lake, IN: Eisenbrauns, 2013.

Lindgren, Barbro. *Histoire du petit monsieur tout seul*. Paris: Bayard, 1995.

Lecerf, Auguste. *Introduction à la dogmatique réformée*. 2 vols. Paris: Editions "Je sers," 1931.

Luther, Martin. *Luther's Small Catechism with Explanation*. St. Louis: Concordia, 2017.

Plato. *Symposium*. Translated with commentary by R. E. Allen. New Haven, CT: Yale University Press, 1993.

Rad, Gerhard von. *Genesis: A Commentary*. The Old Testament Library. Translated by John H. Marks. Philadelphia: Westminster Press, 1973.

Romerowski, Sylvain. "Homme et femme." In *Dictionnaire de théologie biblique*, 630–45. Cléon d'Andran: Excelsis, 2006.

Russell, Bertrand, and Frederick C. Copleston. "A Debate on the Existence of God." In *The Existence of God: A Reader*, edited by John Hick, 167–91. London: Collier MacMillan, 1964.

Sartre Jean-Paul. *Nausea*. Translated by Robert Baldick. Harmondsworth, England: Penguin, 1965.

Thomas Aquinas. *Summa theologiae*. 60 vols. Translated by Thomas Gilby et al. New York: McGraw-Hill, 1964–73.

Tresmontant, Claude. *Études de métaphysique biblique*. Paris: Gabalda, 1955.

———. *The Origins of Christian Philosophy*. Twentieth Century Encyclopedia of Catholicism 11. Translated by Mark Pontifex. New York: Hawthorn, 1963.

Van Fraassen, Bas C. "The World of Empiricism." In *Physics and Our View of the World*, edited by Jan Hilgevoord, 114–34. Cambridge: Cambridge University Press, 1994.

Van Til, Cornelius. *A Survey of Christian Epistemology*. Vol 2. of *In Defense of Biblical Christianity*. Ripon, CA: Den Dulk Christian Foundation, 1969.

Walsh, Brian J., and J. Richard Middleton. *The Transforming Vision: Shaping a Christian World View*. Downers Grove, IL: InterVarsity Press, 1984.

Westermann, Claus. *Genesis*. Biblischer Kommentar Altes Testament 1. Neukirchen-Vluyn: Neukirchener Verlag, 1970.

Winter, Bruce. *Roman Wives, Roman Widows: The Appearance of New Women and the Pauline Communities*. Grand Rapids: Eerdmans, 2003.

Wolters, Albert M. *Creation Regained: Biblical Basics for a Reformational Worldview*. Carlisle, UK: Paternoster, 1996.

NOTES

1. The talk I gave was later published as the article "Se savoir créature" in *Théologie Evangélique* 4 (2005): 45–58. The latter served as the basis for chapters 2, 3, and 7 of this book.

2. Claude Tresmontant, *Etudes de métaphysique biblique* (Paris: Gabalda, 1955), 40.

3. W. G. Lambert, *Babylonian Creation Myths*, Mesopotamian Civilizations 16 (Winona Lake, IN: Eisenbrauns, 2013), 51, 95.

4. Thomas Aquinas, *Summa theologiae* Ia.2.3, trans. Thomas Gilby et al., 60 vols. (New York: McGraw-Hill, 1964–73).

5. Bertrand Russell and Frederick Copleston, "A Debate on the Existence of God," in *The Existence of God: A Reader*, ed. John Hick (London: Collier MacMillan, 1964), 173–74.

6. Jean-Paul Sartre, *Nausea*, trans. Robert Baldick (Harmondsworth, England: Penguin, 1965), 188.

7. Sartre, *Nausea*, 188.

8. Sartre, *Nausea*, 190.

9. Sartre, *Nausea*, 124.

10. Martin Luther, *Luther's Small Catechism with Explanation* (St. Louis, MO: Concordia, 2017), 16.

11. Sartre, *Nausea*, 145–46.

12. Auguste Lecerf, *Introduction à la dogmatique réformée*, vol. 1 (Paris: Editions "Je sers," 1931), 62.

13. Walter Eichrodt, *Theology of the Old Testament*, trans. J. A. Baker, Old Testament Library, 2 vols. (Philadelphia: Westminster John Knox, 1967), 112.

14. Sartre, *Nausea*, 113–14.

15. Paul Clavier, *Dieu sans barbe: vingt et une conversations instructives et amusantes sur la question très disputée de l'existence de Dieu* (Paris: Table Ronde, 2002), 39, quoting the conclusion of Hannah Arendt, *The Origins of Totalitarianism* (Berlin: Schocken, 1951).

16. Based on my translation of the original German, "*Das ewig Unbegreifliche an der Welt ist ihre Begreiflichkeit*" (Albert Einstein, "Physik und Realität," *Franklin Institute Journal* 221 [1936]: 315).

17. Bas C. Van Fraassen, "The World of Empiricism," in *Physics and Our View of the World*, ed. Jan Hilgevoord (Cambridge: Cambridge University Press, 1994), 123.

18. Emmanuel Kant, *Critique of Pure Reason: In Commemoration of the Centenary of Its First Publication*, trans. Max Müller, 2nd ed. (New York: Macmillan, 1907), 102.

19. Cornelius Van Til, *A Survey of Christian Epistemology*, vol. 2 of *In Defense of Biblical Christianity* (Ripon, CA: Den Dulk Christian Foundation, 1969), 203.

20. Pierre Gisel, *La création: essai sur la liberté et la nécessité, l'histoire et la loi, l'homme, le mal et Dieu*, 2nd ed. (Geneva: Labor et Fides, 1987), 170. The author uses the term "realist" in the context of the problem of universals.

21. That is, the Igigi.

22. Stephanie Dalley, *Myths from Mesopotamia: Gilgamesh, The Flood, and Others* (Oxford: Oxford University Press, 1989), 9–15.

23. Identifying the two other rivers mentioned in the text is problematic: What is the Pishon, which flows around Havilah, a mysterious land that abounds in gold and precious stones? And the Gihon, which waters the land of Cush? There are two ways of interpreting these geographical references. One starts from the meaning of the names known with certainty and locates Eden in Mesopotamia. The other interpretation starts from the fact that the country of Cush in the Bible usually (but not always) refers to Nubia, south of Egypt. The Gihon would then be the Nile. If the first branch is identified with the Indus, Eden's river would thereby bring together all the great rivers known in antiquity (Henri Blocher, *In the Beginning: The Opening Chapters of Genesis*, trans. David G. Preston [Downers Grove, IL: InterVarsity, 1984], 116–19; Kenneth Kitchen, *On the Reliability of the Old Testament* [Grand Rapids: Eerdmans, 2003], 429–30).

24. Although it is more commonly said that humans are created "in God's image" (which suggests that God creates them by using himself as a template), the preposition used in the original Hebrew is better translated, in this context, by "as" or "so as to be." It is

therefore humans who are the visible image of God (Blocher, *In the Beginning*, 85). My treatment of the theme of the image of God is indebted to Blocher, chapter 4.

25. John Calvin, *Institutes of the Christian Religion*, ed. John T. McNeill, trans. Ford Lewis Battles, The Library of Christian Classics, 2 vols. (Louisville, KY: Westminster John Knox, 2011), I.XV.

26. Calvin, *Institutes* II.II.1.

27. Blocher, *In the Beginning*, 89.

28. Blocher, *In the Beginning*, 89.

29. "Elle a fait un bébé toute seule," from the album *Entre gris clair et gris foncé*, 1987.

30. Blocher, *In the Beginning*, 126.

31. Blocher, *In the Beginning*, 133.

32. See chapter 4.

33. See note 23.

34. "Vivre cent vies," from the album *Fredericks Goldman Jones*, 1990.

35. Hans Urs von Balthasar, *The Truth of the World*, vol. 1 of *Theo-Logic: Theological Logical Theory*, trans. Adrian J. Walker (San Francisco: Ignatius Press, 2000), 190.

36. The expression is inspired by Barbro Lindgren's children's book *The Story of the Little Old Man*, whose title in French is *Histoire du petit monsieur tout seul* (Paris: Bayard, 1995).

37. Karl Barth, *Church Dogmatics* III.1, trans. J. W. Edwards, O. Bussey, and H. Knight (Edinburgh: T&T Clark, 1958), 196.

38. Plato, *Symposium*, trans. R. E. Allen (New Haven, CT: Yale University Press, 1993), 130–32.

39. James Robert Boyd, *The Westminster Shorter Catechism, with Analysis, Scriptural Proofs, Explanatory and Practical Inferences, and Illustrative Anecdotes* (Philadelphia: Presbyterian Publication Committee, 1854), 19.

40. Blocher, *In the Beginning*, 99–100, quoting Matthew Henry (1708–1710), who seems to follow Thomas Aquinas.

41. Bruce Winter, *Roman Wives, Roman Widows: The Appearance of New Women and the Pauline Communities* (Grand Rapids: Eerdmans, 2003), chapter 6.

42. For a balanced in-depth treatment of the question of female ministry in church, see Henri Blocher, "Women, Ministry and the Gospel. Hints for a New Paradigm ?", in M. Husbands and T. Larsen, ed. *Women, Ministry and the Gospel. Exploring New Paradigms* (Downers Grove, IVP Academic, 2007), 239–49.

43. Sylvain Romerowski, "Homme et femme," *Dictionnaire de théologie biblique* (Cléon d'Andran: Excelsis, 2006), 631.

44. Deliberation presupposes some kind of inner structure, allowing the person to take some critical distance and reflect on their choice (cf. 2 Samuel 24:14). But how could such a split of personality be possible if God was just [or: only] the Absolute One.

45. Blocher, *In the Beginning*, 104–5.

46. See pages 116–17.

47. Gnosticism refers to syncretistic religious movements that combined elements of Christianity, Greek philosophy, and Eastern religions. It was characterized by a strongly dualistic perspective in which matter and spirit were opposed to one another. Gnostic belief systems reached their peak in the second and third centuries AD, but some elements of them were already perceptible at the time the New Testament was being written, in the first century.

48. Jean Ansaldi, " 'Célibat pour Christ' et sexualité," *Études Théologiques et Religieuses* 67 (1992): 411–14.

49. Calvin, *Institutes* II.VIII.

SUBJECT & AUTHOR INDEX

A

Abortion 67
Abstinence (sexual) 107, 139,
    141–42
Anorexia 78
Art 37, 68–69, 154–55
Asceticism 66, 87, 142
Atheism 10, 56
Atrahasis 45–47, 50, 73
Augustine (Saint) 65

B

Babylonian Creation Story 4–7
Bacon, Francis 154
Balthasar, Hans Urs von 106
Barth, Karl 75, 115
Big Bang xiv
Birth control 66
Blessing 28, 52–54, 63–79, 85–87,
    100, 102–3, 108, 120, 137,
    151–52, 156
Body 20, 21, 37, 50-53, 58, 77,
    101–2, 116–17, 137, 140

Bulimia 78

C

Calvin, John 55, 75, 157
Childlessness 67
Clothing 20, 162
Contingency 15–19
Copleston, Frederick 16

D

Death 51, 93–94, 103, 107
Dependency (creational) 10, 22,
    76, 88, 108, 150, 151
Differentiation (sexual) 29, 57, 67,
    101, 115, 116–17, 118, 125,
    127–28, 133–34, 137–41
Discrimination 57, 103
Divorce 135–37
Dominion over nature 36, 51,
    54–57, 68–72, 78, 81, 119,
    125
Duality of body and soul 50, 58

E

Eating disorders 78
Ecology 35, 70–71
Einstein, Albert 38
Emancipation 123–124
End (man's chief end) 119, 152
Enuma Elish 4–7
Environment 49, 69–70

Equality of the sexes 121–22,
    123–24
Evolution (theory of) xiv, 6, 58

F

Faculties (rational) 55, 56, 68
Faithfulness 106
Fall 70–74, 76, 80, 123, 138, 162
Fear of God 89–91
Food 20, 48, 72–81, 119, 149
Freud, Sigmund 118

G

Goldmann, Jean-Jacques 67,
    103–6

H

Harmony of creation 31, 36, 58, 76,
    78–80, 122, 147, 148, 163
Homosexuality 128
Hume, David 38

I

Idolatry 9–10, 22, 128
Illness 67, 103
Image of God xi, xiv, 53, 55–59,
    63, 65–66, 68, 71, 114, 115,
    119–21, 129, 153
Infertility 67, 137
Innocence (original) 51, 55, 161–62

K

Kant, Emmanuel 40–41

L

Laws of nature 8, 34, 38
Luther, Martin 19–20

M

Marriage 65–66, 89, 106, 113,
    133–41
Mind (human) 39–40, 58
Morality 8, 85–94
Myth of the androgynous human
    115–17
Mythology 4–9, 45–47, 73

N

Necessity 15–16

O

Order (creational) 27–31, 34,
    35–37, 67, 118, 120–26, 129,
    137

P

Perversions (sexual) 65, 87, 128,
    138
Plato 116–17, 137
Pleasure 86
Polygamy 139
Polytheism 4, 31
Prayer xv, 10–11

Procreation 64–68, 119, 125, 137,
    152, 161
Prostitution 140
Providence 76, 149–50

R

Rest 28, 48, 147–59
Ricœur, Paul 75
Russell, Bertrand 16

S

Sabbath 48, 147–59
Salvation 52–52, 77, 119–20, 153,
    156–59
Sartre, Jean-Paul 17–19, 21, 32–34
Self-sufficiency 9, 48
Sexuality 55–56, 133–42
Sin 36, 57, 65, 67, 73, 78, 80–81, 92,
    100, 102–3, 107, 118, 128,
    137, 148, 151
Singleness 66, 141–42
Spirit (human) 6, 50, 52
Status of women 115–29

T

Technology 35, 68, 70–71, 100,
    154
Thomas Aquinas 15–16
Totalitarianism 37, 90
Trinity 31, 114, 125–27

U

Unemployment 69

V

Van Fraasen, Bas 39
Vaux, Roland de 75
Vegetarianism 80–81

Vocation 36, 41, 51, 55, 57, 63–64,
    67–71, 100, 119, 121,
    125–26, 129, 137, 141, 152,
    159

W

Westminster Shorter Catechism
    (1648) 119
Work 46, 48, 68–72, 158–59

SCRIPTURE INDEX

Old Testament

Genesis

1	28–29, 48
1:1	3, 54
1:2	127
1:3	10
1:11	56, 99
1:12	56
1:21	54
1:22	53
1:26	59, 119, 127
1:27	54, 56, 67, 115, 119
1:28	36, 51, 53, 54, 63, 64, 68, 119, 137
1:29	48, 73, 78, 119
1:30	48, 78, 119
1:31	28, 148, 153
2	48, 57, 120
2:1–3	48, 148
2:4	49
2:5	51
2:7	6, 50, 53
2:8	48
2:9	48
2:15	36, 51, 69, 99
2:16	51, 85
2:17	85
2:18	113
2:19	53
2:20	114
2:23	118, 122
2:24	66, 122, 134

2:25 .... 147, 162
3 52
3:2–3 122
3:6 ....73, 87
3:16 .... 123, 125
3:17–19 ....70, 76, 125
3:18 80
3:21 162
3:22 .... 51, 74
4:1 65
4:2 80
4:4 80
4:13–14 100
9:3 80
16:29–30 139

Exodus

20:8–11 155
31:12–17 156
35:2 155

Numbers

32:29 69

Deuteronomy

1:39 75
5:14 158

6:4–5 91
8:3 77
30:15–18 93–94

2 Samuel

14:17 75

1 Kings

3:9 75

Esther

7:8 69

Job

28:25–27 30
38:4–6 30
38:25 30
38:39 81
39:27–30 81
41:14–17 81

Psalms

19:1 152
33:6 31
68:5 68
93:1 30
96:10 30

104:27–30 149
115:8 22
115:16 108
119:89–91 30
127:3 167

Proverbs

31:10–31 125

Ecclesiastes

5:1 108
9:7 77
12:13 89

Isaiah

7:15–16 75
11:6 80
44:9 22
65:25 80

Jeremiah

34:11 69

Zechariah

12:1 50
14:20–21 163

New Testament

Matthew

4:10 11

19:3–9 .... 135, 136
22:39 57

John

1:3 31

5:17–19 148–49

Acts

17:24–25 45
20:7 158

Romans

1:20 16
1:22 9
1:25 9
1:25–27 128
14:5 156

1 Corinthians

4:7 19
6:16–18 140
7:2 139
7:26 66
10:31 ....79, 163, 170

11:3 .... 121, 126, 127
11:3–16 124
11:8–9 121
11:11–12 122
14:33 31
14:33–40 124
16:2 158

Ephesians

5:25 123
5:31–32 127

Colossians

2:17 156
3:10 53

1 Timothy

2:13 121
2:15 124

4:4 66

Hebrews

1:3 31
4:1–10 153
4:9 151
9:27 103

1 Peter

3:7 119

Revelation

1:10 158
4:11 xi
21:1–22:5 100
21:2........................... 154
22:14 94

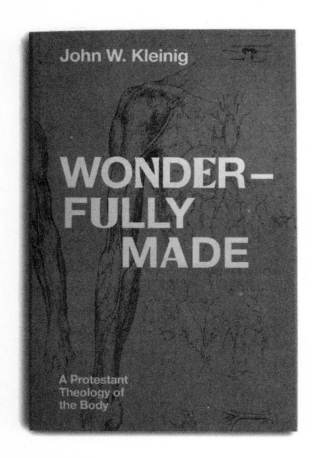

ALSO AVAILABLE FROM LEXHAM PRESS

Think deeply about God's word and the body

Visit lexhampress.com to learn more